The Warming of Winter

Maxine Dowd Jensen

The Warming of Winter

Abingdon   Nashville

THE WARMING OF WINTER

Library of Congress Cataloging in Publication Data

Jensen, Maxine Dowd, 1919-
   The warming of winter.
   1. Widows—United States. I. Title.

HQ1058.5.U5J45   301.42'86   76-49941

ISBN 0-687-44009-2

Chapter 1 uses material from the author's article "Widow—Take Heart," which appeared in *The Evangelical Beacon*, March 4, 1975. Reprinted by permission, *Evangelical Beacon*, magazine of the Evangelical Free Church of America.

MANUFACTURED BY THE PARTHENON PRESS AT
NASHVILLE, TENNESSEE, UNITED STATES OF AMERICA

In Memory Of
Cliff

Preface

To you,

On the night of the crisis in my widowhood I scribbled some words on paper. The first creative words I'd written since my marriage over thirteen years before. Sometimes I've wondered if God removed my most precious possession so that I would again lift my pen. Immediately after this thought crossed my mind I knew it was unfair to God.

Unfair because I had planned to write again. Warning my husband that—come retirement—I intended to spend four hours a day, three days a week writing. No telephone or doorbell answering. Not even time out for a kiss.

Therefore it seems fitting to me that my first writing after my crisis night was a "widow" article. A revised, first-person version was the second piece of my writing to sell. Now it has expanded into a book. My first book.

A book in which God is my helper. Just as he has been in every important thing I've attempted. And some things not so important. A partnership that began one bright October day when I was thirteen and on the brink of a new life, my Christian life.

Since that fall day people have told me a number of things. Many times I was a free thinker. I didn't agree.

7

Now, many widows tell me—and perhaps you, too—"It gets worse, not better, as time goes by."

Don't you believe it! As the song says, "It ain't necessarily so."

My greatest desire and prayer for you is that through this book you will find the map leading to a richer, happier road ahead. A more wonderful life than you ever dreamed possible as you said good-bye to the earthly body of your "other half."

I have found it so. I am not extraordinary. I am not unique. Other than God, I have no outstanding assets. But he is in my heart, and he is enough for me. And he can be for you.

With him we can determine to put aside our "widow blues" and live again and reach for the stars.

Love in him,
Maxine Dowd Jensen

Contents

1

He Died–I Died

It isn't easy to watch a man slowly die. Neither is it easy when he is suddenly cut off. In either case, if you are his wife, you die, too. I did.

At 4:15 P.M., on Tuesday, December 12, 1972, my life stopped. I became a widow. Oh, I was still breathing, walking, talking. But living seemed no longer a part of me.

I did the usual things. I contacted the minister. I picked out the songs, the singers, the undertaker, the casket.

It should have helped that the undertaker was a friend, as were the organist and the singers. It should have been a consolation that the minister had known me since my late teens, had sorrowed with me when my parents died and rejoiced with me at my marriage. But it didn't.

I was alone.

My husband's younger daughter, strong and wonderful, was there. So was her fiancé, helpful and kind. My son-in-law was there like a firm rock. But I felt abandoned.

All the things I had to do, I did. All the friends who pressed my hand and murmured words of sympathy and assurance were appreciated. Yet, I was isolated. Apart from them. Alone. More so than ever before.

11

Friends once thought it very strange that I felt becoming an old maid wasn't the worst thing that could happen to a woman. Then they were perplexed because I wasn't worried about stepping into a household as stepmother to a teen-aged girl. Some predicted I would never be happy in the denomination of my future husband.

At those times I was optimistic but not because I was either stupid or unusual. My optimism was based on my confidence in a compassionate and infinitely loving God. This confidence and this optimism have never been lost to me for long.

Though the numbness following parting may, for some, continue for an indefinite period, my new breakthrough to life and living again began the night I remembered.

I remembered a day in October. It was a shiny, bright day. We had gone out to Maple Lake.

At first I sat in the car. I watched him start walking toward the water's edge. Something about the droop of his shoulders stirred my heart, and I knew, though it was chilly, that I must go with him.

Quickly I caught up. We linked our hands and scuffed our feet through the fallen leaves. We sat at a picnic table and watched a boat go out from the dock and another come in.

I noticed an older couple. The man threw his fishing line out into the water and slowly reeled it in. A young father and son tried to catch a fish, while a younger sister climbed about a disfigured tree.

Then the teen-aged couple came. Holding hands as we had done, but chatting gaily.

I stole a glance at him. The only man I'd ever loved. What were his thoughts? The usual smile and happy light in his eyes were missing. Had he been thinking, as had I, that this was his last look at autumn? His last glimpse of brilliant leaves? Our final visit to Maple Lake?

Suddenly the wind forced its chill through my bright sweater and my heart. Warning of winter? Of death?

Soon we rose. Our fingers gently touched, then clasped together tightly. As if this touch, this grasp, would hold us together—forever.

Slowly we walked back to the car. We sat there for a time—watching the wind play with the leaves, watching the sun's fading rays catch every color.

Our hands and arms were still entwined. But I dared not look. I dared not find in his eyes what I knew to be in mine.

The motor's roar broke the silence. In a fast-slipping moment the lake, the winding road, the colored leaves were all behind us.

Then winter came.

For him, somewhere, was another spring, a new beginning. For me, now, there was only the cold, chill lonesomeness of winter.

That night, as I remembered, the tears finally came. Slowly at first. Then hot and torrential. I cried until 4:00 A.M.

If there is a crisis in widowhood, that night was mine. When morning came I knew I could no longer remain in the limbo I'd been in since his death. Neither could I look back.

I looked up.

God had never failed me before. I realized he hadn't failed me now. True, he hadn't healed my husband. However, through his mercy, my husband had been saved much of the agony and downward progression a doctor friend (at my insistence) had described to me. God had called him home. When he went to meet his Savior and Friend, he had said, "Oh, God. You know that I love you."

As the sun rose on the morning of my remembrance, I thanked God. I started back from there.

2

Another Spring

"What would you like for breakfast, Jack?" I asked my son-in-law on Sunday, the day after the funeral.

"A fried egg, over," he replied.

Such a simple thing. Yet, I'd never fried an egg.

Oh, we often had them on weekends; but my husband was the breakfast cook, while I dashed up and down the steps putting clothes in the washer, running the vacuum, and all the other tasks always awaiting a working wife.

I stood there, the frying pan in one hand, the egg in the other.

How many times in the future would I find myself standing the same way? How many things had I never done? How many things had I taken for granted?

One of those taken-for-granted, habitual things for me is church. Later that morning, as I stood in the narthex and shook the snow from my coat, I saw Claudine, another widow, approaching.

"What are you doing here?" she bluntly asked.

Softly I replied, "It's Sunday. I belong here."

Women approach life alone in many different ways. Before I was married, my heart was stirred as I read how Catherine Marshall faced living again. Now I am doing it.

15

The first, the most important thing for me, as it should be for you, is to continue to yield your life to God. He is aware of all your problems. He knows the reason why. Even so, you can tell him, "Lord, I'm unhappy. I don't understand why. But, you never do anything without a good reason. Help me. Lead me. And, God, use me. Show me the way."

When my mother died, it was the first time in my life I was responsible only for myself. I could take any job God wanted me to fill. Go any place he led me. No one would suffer but me. Marriage was his leading then.

Now I have still another chance—another exciting opportunity to follow in his direction. I am praying and you can too. He will not fail either of us.

Some people tell me, "Oh, you're young. You were only married thirteen years." They say it's different when you're older or have a thirty-fifth or fortieth anniversary behind you.

Perhaps it is. But loss of a loved mate is one of the most trying experiences of life. At any age. To male or female.

However, how you face it depends on you, and you alone. How willing or how able are you to adjust? It's not how old you are. Or how long you've lived together. Or even how much you have loved each other.

A young woman I knew, suddenly lost her husband. They were a very attractive couple. Greatly in love. They had two small sons under school age. A comfortable older home was theirs. He had an excellent job.

When he died, she was heartbroken. This is normal. However, she began to drink, to forget her boys. She became an alcoholic, took a leech into her home. She died within two years. She did this to herself, and it left an indelible mark on her boys.

Another widow, mother of five, equally young, equally attractive, equally loving and loved, moved to a smaller house after her husband, inexplicably, killed himself. She took a waitress job, joined with her boys at the altar rail for their baptism, and, a number of years later, married again.

One person, old or young, refuses to face reality. Another will look up to our compassionate Father and live.

Some widows shut themselves in. Won't answer the door or the telephone. Others run madly as if to obliterate any time when they will be alone, any guilt feelings. There are individuals who throw inhibitions to the wind. And there are even those who try to sap the life's blood from their children by demanding constant attention.

Widows are usually older women; yet, reactions are much the same. When the first numbing days are past, you will wonder what to do. Everyone will tell you to keep busy. This is good advice, but how should you busy yourself?

Start with things you know.

I began singing again. Really practicing. While married, unless I had a special engagement for a solo, I rarely vocalized. Except for choir rehearsal, I seldom sang.

It wasn't easy at first. So many songs I picked up were love songs. The treble cleff sign would grow grotesque, the lines would waver like quivering whitecaps on a beach. The words would become a blur sticking in my throat.

Carefully I'd put the music aside and wait for another day.

Singing is a natural part of life for me. Since I was thirteen I've been in junior choirs, senior choirs, the chorus where I worked in Chicago, the Swedish Choral Club, and others. So, though I dropped out of choir during the last months of my husband's illness, the first Friday of the New Year found me back in my place. Sometimes I thought I heard his booming bass behind me. I looked. Then tried to cover my embarrassment. Even now, almost four years later, I can never approach the portals of heaven in "Open My Eyes" without tears skittering down my cheeks. I can't sing "Wonderful Guy" from South Pacific without a lump rising in my throat. But it is getting easier.

Some of the things you begin again will bring you the same sad rememberings. But start in. Temporarily stop, if you must; only be sure you do not allow the desire to disappear, to be unexplored.

I'm writing again. It's fun. It's time-consuming. It's what I've wanted and haphazardly tried to do since I sold my first poem at age eight or nine. (By the way, I still have the quarter I earned then, but not the poem.) Is it what God would have me do? At this point I answer yes.

I'm still praying. I'm continuing to seek his leading. I often murmur, "What more will ye have me do?"

All of us possess a minimum of one talent—at least one thing we can share with others. Begin to use it, polish it, make a present of it to others. God plans special things for each one of us.

Maybe you are as impatient as I. It's hard to wait for

God's leading. Many times, it's even difficult to be sure of his direction. In the meantime, do other things. New things.

One day, reading the weekly paper, I saw that bowling leagues were forming. I called. "I'm new in the area," I said. "I like bowling but have never been in a league. Could I qualify?" That first winter was so much fun, I signed up for the summer league.

One young widow I know did the same thing. She said she began to look forward to her night out with adults as a relief from constantly conversing with two small children. Some new clothes and a fresh hair style brightened that bowling day.

Join something. Even if it's only one thing done once a month, it's a start to living again.

In our town we have an arts and crafts building. For a small fee and your service as a clerk once a month, you can bring anything you make and sell it. The group receives a percentage, and you get the rest.

Many women find handwork a profitable use of time and talent. It took me twenty years to finish my first afghan, so you can guess how good I am at this sort of thing. However, at my neighbors' insistence, I entered a crocheted cape and a shell in the county fair.

Later, entering the handcraft room, I saw my orange sherbet cape. It looked mighty good with the royal blue ribbon on it. Then I saw the gold shell. I clapped my hand to my mouth and began to giggle. It had a blue ribbon, too.

Then I looked up and murmured, "Mother, I'm in your class now." You see, she always entered the Missouri

State Fair. The year we moved to Chicago she took five cakes and won four firsts and one second.

One widow, previously superb at cooking and baking, has closed her mind. She works full time and, if not invited out, will watch television and sleep. No longer does she serve even simple dinners to close friends. No longer does she light the burner under the coffeepot to share a cup.

I spent several days with her recently, and we watched fourteen hours of TV. Not much, you say? If it's fourteen straight hours? All in one day and into the early morn? I had to be there to believe it.

She always has the energy to get up at 4:00 A.M. if preparing for an outdoor breakfast get-together. This strength mysteriously ebbs away every Sunday at church time.

She is often lonely and unhappy. And wonders why. I love her. My heart goes out to her. Many friends have tried to help, but she turns her back on all suggestions. Unless it's a suggestion to "go."

This situation is doubly sad because she has one of the prettiest singing voices I have ever heard. She can play the piano. She's a top-notch musician. But she is no longer interested in using her talents for God. She seems to be blaming him, punishing him, for taking away her loved one.

It's hard to be alone. Don't let anyone tell you differently. So—force yourself to do things. Some days the inspiration, the desire, will not be there. Begin anyway. If it still doesn't come, quit. Most of the time it will be like singing and writing. Once the phlegm is gone, once the ink starts to flow, things move, brighten. Your soul is lifted.

Loneliness is not often a problem if you wrap yourself in a book. I curl up in my big high-backed chair in front of my fireplace and, in a moment, I'm transported to a different place, a different world. Like me, you may rarely cry over your own misfortunes, but you can weep copiously and without shame over the trials of others. Fictional characters give almost as much love and laughter as real people.

How-to books, inspirational ones, light Gothic novels, and such, fill up my reading hours. Sandburg's *Lincoln*, all six volumes, has been an education and enjoyment for me. Shakespeare gives me almost as many inspirational passages as my Bible. Some poetry, such as "Invictus" and "Seein' Things at Night," possesses rhythm and a feeling worth reading about.

Books open a marvelous door. They bring the wide-eyed thrill of childhood and new adventure into your life. It's a wonderful world.

As I say this, the library has just called me about a book I requested. On the coffee table in my den I have exactly twenty-seven unread paperbacks. I'm reading September issues of my magazines and it's January. My neighbor teases me because I give her my year-old issues to read. But they are all there, waiting for me. And for her. Ready to take me away from my troubles and any sad personal thoughts.

Old things, familiar duties are good. However, widowhood can mean adventure, can reveal the thrill of something new.

My only complaint about my chosen place of residence is the absence of a nearby college or university. But I've just discovered that even "old" ladies can enroll in summer courses in the U.S.A. or on foreign soil. The University of Oklahoma has quite a correspondence school encompassing both high school and college subjects. I plan to check these out. What about you?

What we really want to do is usually possible.

A widow I know lost a chauffeur when her next-door neighbor moved. Though a driver herself, she had come to rely—or impose?—on her friend. Soon after the neighbor moved, because the widow desired to go places, she began driving herself.

What fascinates you should be explored. I promise it will often result in new friends.

Volunteers are always needed—in your church, in your community, and wherever there are people. Happiness is often just being needed.

At one time I donated my Saturday mornings to the Rural Bible Crusade office in Wheaton, Illinois. At another point in my life I was privileged to work with the Easter sunrise committee that sponsored the Easter sunrise services in Chicago's Soldier Field. Now I should like to man a hot-line for the American Cancer Society. I've contacted them, and I hope they will have one soon in my community.

Children, orphans, the retarded, and those in day-care centers need you. Your love and your faith. Or sign up to be a foster grandparent, a teacher's assistant . . .

A married friend gives freely of her time to a home for

the aged. She took me with her to see if I might be interested in helping there. I do not believe I could do as she does. It would prove too depressing for me.

Funny isn't it, how differently we are made? I can try to cheer up and listen to a terminally ill cancer victim, and speak a word for Jesus; yet I quiver inside at the sight of a poor old person twisted in a wheelchair or lying immobile from a stroke. However, this may be a place of service for you.

Some widowed friends are applying for admittance to L.P.N. training. If accepted, they will have a lucrative new profession as practical nurses. Money, or the lack of it, sometimes plagues a widow. You might want to try nursing.

Neighbors and friends often welcome a helping hand, a shoulder to cry on, a never-tell-a-soul confidant. Could it be that you'd fill the bill?

While I was married, especially in the four years when my husband fought cancer, I watched widowed friends. I did not give up hope God would heal him until five days before he died. Then I stood at that hospital window, looked out at the miserable gray, spitty December gloom, and said to myself, "Max, you've got to face it. He isn't going to get better." But I observed widows. I thought of things I would or would not do, should I be in their shoes. (This is normal. My husband did it, too, between his first wife's cancer operation and her death two and a half years later in an automobile accident.)

I determined first that I would never blame God. I might, as I have done, ask him Why, but I knew I would try very hard never to be bitter or reject him. After all, he has been with me in every one of my joys as well as my sorrows. He is my strong defense. And which of us hasn't asked him Why?

"Max, you've got a direct pipeline to God," my husband used to say. For some reason the pipeline didn't work during his last illness. Rather, it didn't work the way we hoped. But it still worked.

My husband was spared many of the miseries an acquaintance experienced who suffered the same thing at the same time. God did hear, and he answered in his own way.

It is not quite enough to send the incense of our prayers upward, revive old interests, and kindle new ones. These are fundamentally self-centered things. If we are to be truly happy in our new state, we must turn our thoughts outward.

My husband died just before Christmas. Three invitations for the holiday were extended to me, only one of which included my young daughter. What should I do? Waking early one morning, tossing on my bed, I decided.

One of my friends never invites anyone. She says she can't do it now that her husband is gone. Could I? Of course I could!

For me it is usually easier to have a talk with myself and then plunge in. I'm inclined to procrastinate. Putting off things I dread to do only makes them that much worse.

As soon as it was a reasonable hour I called my younger daughter. I invited her and her boyfriend. Then I telephoned some friends whose son would be at his in-laws.

I took the plunge. And—it wasn't bad.

I don't have many dinner parties, but "coffee and . . . " isn't hard. Invite your friends. Don't expect always to be invited to their houses; it wasn't so when you were a couple. Gifts and dinner out are pleasant "thank yous," but nothing replaces the cozy cup of coffee and the chat around your own table. They'll like it, and it is very good for you.

Man talk is one of the things I miss in widowhood. You probably will, too, unless you're blessed with male relatives close at hand. Boys and men have always been favorites of mine. Better liked by me than most girls and women. I always wanted sons, but I never really cared if I had daughters—though I shouldn't want to part with the two stepdaughters I now have.

So invite couples, old friends and new. Invite two couples at a time. The man doesn't feel isolated, the wife doesn't think you are out to snare her husband, and five is not an awesome number to entertain.

Look up other widows. If you drive, take them out with you occasionally. Even if you don't drive, it will mean a great deal to them to get together with you. Even a telephone call is pleasant to receive.

Occasionally invite younger people over—children of your friends or some you have met. They can put pizzazz in your life, profit by your experience and your faith, and become good friends.

If you like children you can plan cookie bakes, babysit

for a young widow, or enable a harried young mother to have a little free time.

Some of the most revealing, interesting conversations I've ever enjoyed have been with nine-year-old boys. It's astounding how much they see and how profound are their minds. They understand and question and seek answers much more than most people realize. Teen-agers need an adult who is detached. Someone they can confide in. Someone who won't tell but will listen objectively and counsel them. I've found this a fruitful opportunity for God.

Last summer—with fear and trembling—I agreed to be a counselor at a church camp for seventh and eighth graders. I'd been a counselor for a teen-aged youth group before my marriage, but this is a new and supposedly different generation.

I read everything I could. I listened to the crepe-hanging of teachers and a former camp counselor. I arrived at the sad conclusion I was going armed with only two weapons. I like teen-agers, and I love God.

I had a ball! I relived my own eager youth. I played baseball, volleyball, ping-pong. I sang. I went fishing with some of the boys. I swam. And, after lights-out, I had heart-to-heart talks with my cabin crew. In the dark we discussed many things. Spiritual things. Things that trouble the current teen-ager. Questions and answers flew back and forth between the bunks.

There was only one problem. After living most of my life in the North, I couldn't always understand the Southern accent. Did you know that if you have kin named "Pal" it is spelled "Powell"? I didn't.

Some of these young people write to me now, and I eagerly look forward to their letters. They are new friends I cherish.

God says that to have friends we must show ourselves to be friendly. Life is full of friends—and meaning and joy and contentment—if you seek God's leading. Follow him, and you too can begin to revel in another spring.

3

They Hurt, Too

We faced each other from identical blue crushed-velvet chairs. She picked at imaginary lint on her long skirt and crossed her legs. I thought it would be easier for her to talk now that she had married again. Then I wondered as her tear-washed voice began. Softly. Haltingly.

"It was . . . it was the suppertimes that were hardest at first. I lived in that big, impersonal apartment building. But, for all its impersonality, you could always hear doors open. Could hear 'Hon, I'm home.' From every apartment but mine. Sometimes I even thought I heard the key in my lock."

She paused a moment, plucked again at her immaculate skirt, and recrossed her legs.

"It hurt. I couldn't help saying again and again, 'Why me, Lord?' But no answer came."

She looked up then.

"At the funeral parlor I heard people whisper, 'Poor thing,' because I was pregnant. Then, later, people said I was lucky to have the children for company. Company? What real company are a three-year-old boy and a baby? A baby Nick would never see?"

She surreptitiously wiped the tip of her index finger across her right cheekbone to halt the sliding tear.

"Oh, Nicky, the baby, was good. He laughed and gurgled and almost made me forget sometimes. Then Tim would do something. Like the day he scratched up a beautiful picture of Nick. When I grabbed it from him he shouted in his baby voice, 'I hate him. He went away and left me. He didn't even kiss me goodbye.'

"Nick always tossed Tim high and kissed him whenever he left for work. It was Nick who had the last goodnight, the last kiss for him each evening. They had just started to be real pals."

Slowly she went on.

"I guess that's why I finally accepted Rita's invitation to join them for their cocktail hour. Anything for a diversion. But I'm not very good at drinking. I become either lightheaded or very sick. The night I found myself trying to stuff cereal into Nicky's ear ended that. It wasn't any solution anyway. I knew it when I began.

"It seems that I had just started to recover when Dad died. Even more suddenly than Nick. And I was alone again."

Her long, tapered fingers smoothed out the unwrinkled skirt.

"That's when I began to cry again. Every night. I tried sleeping on Nick's side of the bed, and that helped some; but many nights I sat, his picture in my hands, and just looked and cried.

"It was such a night when a neighbor who'd become a friend came over. Then she brusquely said, 'Are you going to sit there all night feeling sorry for yourself, or will you come over for a few hours?'

"It was as though she had slapped me square in the face. It's what I call 'laying it on the line.' I needed it.

"As I thought of her words later on, it came to me. I was feeling sorry for myself. So preoccupied over my loss I'd even forgotten the meaning of our minister's words during the funeral service. My husband had attained what we are all struggling for. To be with our Creator and at last have peace. Nick was the lucky one. He already had it made."

Looking over at me with that heavenly smile, she continued. "It was then I returned to church, where I should have been from the beginning."

The smile faded from her eyes, and she became very serious.

"You know, there should be some guidelines for the surviving parent on how to help the child. Tim pulled up neighbors' flowers, ran away several times, and he still grabs at life. Though he loves my husband, he acts as though he doesn't want to get too close in case he'll disappear, too, just as his dad and his granddad did.

"I'll admit I didn't understand him. Why he was doing those things. I tried to shield him. During the wake I left him with friends who had children. But I think we should let them be as much a part of what is happening as we can. Within reason. After all, it's happening to them, too."

I understood what she meant. My young stepdaughter, though fourteen instead of three, had exhibited some of the symptoms of this traumatic hurt after her mother was killed in an auto accident. She acted as though she didn't care (she cared too much). She beat a path between the refrigerator and the TV (then was unhappy because of her excess weight). She closed out her dad, me, and everyone else (loneliness increased; so did her unhappiness).

She tried to hurt those who loved her the most. When I baked a pie, the next day she baked a cake. She would appear at the supper table coated with makeup. She knew her father hated it and thought her too young to wear it.

The day we arrived home to find a lovely cake on the countertop I thought perhaps I was finally getting through to her. It was my birthday.

When her dad said, "Let's cut the cake," she replied, "Oh, I'm taking that over to Dorothy's. It's her mother's birthday tomorrow."

What can we do to ease the hurts of our children, our stepchildren?

You wouldn't expect a funeral director to be of assistance here, but Marjorie was pleasantly surprised. It was one of the brighter notes of that trying time.

Eight-year-old Keith stood and looked at his dad. He stared a long time. Then he changed his position and again gazed at him. The funeral director, who has three small children of his own, began to talk to him. He mentioned the clothes Keith's dad was wearing. "What good taste your father had."

"Look at your dad's hands, Keith. They are fine, strong, capable ones. He worked hard with them to make a living for you and your mom." Then he gave Keith a plastic bee from the flowers. "You can keep this if you like," he said.

Later, at home, Keith remarked he could only see half of his daddy. This was mentioned to the undertaker, and he asked Marjorie to bring a pair of shoes. The next day the director explained why the lower half was closed. Then he moved the floral piece and opened it so Keith could see his daddy's legs and shoes.

The minister also talked to Keith. He explained to him that he could someday go to be with his dad.

Keith was lucky. Many children have no one who gives them straight answers. They are left with their fears, their imaginings, their hurt.

Children are trusting, but they are uncanny in picking out an adult lie. They sense many things. They are much brighter and more discerning than many adults realize.

In my experience, I've found if you take time to talk to them they understand far more than we often think, reason clearly even when not given all the facts, and ask thoughtful, probing questions if allowed to do so. Therefore—let's be truthful with them.

A pediatrics professor says it is important to help children understand the meaning of living and not living. For an example, you can discuss the death of a pet.

Children from three to five have difficulty assimilating the meaning of death. They will be apt to think it is like sleeping. As they grow older they become more knowledgeable.

It is important to distinguish between death and just sleeping or the child may exhibit a fear of going to bed at night. His imaginative powers are great. It is important that he not conjure up fearful ideas.

From ages six to nine the child may also be scared of the dark, but he is ready to enter into new experiences. The death of a loved one is one of these and should be explained to him.

Older children tend toward hero worship. If a father or a mother dies during this period in a child's life it may shatter an image of immortality for him. However, it is also the age when children are inquisitive and want facts—an age when death is more easily understood.

The early teen-aged years signal an emotional period. This is the time when most decisions are made for Christ. The salvation experience and the entry into heaven for the Christian can be tied together.

A child's seeming indifference is saying, "I just can't believe it." So are his tantrums, withdrawal, and so forth. He is crying out, "I hurt, too."

Sometimes just a little togetherness will help calm and reassure a child. Nothing equals the togetherness of eating with one another. If it can be arranged, breakfast is the ideal hour to get the day headed in the right direction. Start with a prayer, use a meditation book, or read directly from God's Word. Begin the day as pleasantly as possible. This will help all of you face an alien world—this time together when each is confident of the love of the others.

Let the children help. Even the smallest can put placemats or napkins on the table. Though children may sometimes fret at the tasks, these things can knit the family closer.

You have to keep going when you have a child or a job, or both.

A good nun told one widow, "God is going to send you

blessed distractions." And, sure enough, he did. Her son had a minor accident. The tile in the bathroom over the tub fell down. The water heater broke. And the basement flooded. Now she can look back and laugh. At the time, she surely didn't thank God for those distractions.

When you have children you may wish to include them in all your social activities, or you may desire a regular night out. If you are honest with them and have enjoyable times with one another, don't feel guilty about wanting to get away occasionally. As a widow once said, "You need to talk to adults, too."

Keep the lines of communications open between yourself and your child. Be honest and truthful. Share your sadness, your joys, your remembrances, the family's needs.

And tune them in on the communications line to God. Help them know that God listens and cares. As he helps you, he will also come to their aid.

4

Valley of Decision

For some people decisions are easy. For most of us they involve listening, weighing, waiting, and praying.

As my mother lay in her casket, friends came with questions and advice. It didn't change much when I stood beside my husband. Probably it was the same for you.

Many good-intentioned people offer all kinds of ideas. Relatives and children often give advice. But you, only you, should make the final decisions.

"Wait on the Lord," the psalmist says. "Be of good courage, and he shall strengthen thine heart: wait, I say, on the Lord."

Shakespeare once said, "Give every man thine ear but few thy voice. Heed each man's counsel but reserve thy judgment."

Pray. Listen. Weigh. Wait. God already knows our need. Before we even call. But don't you think he is pleased when we talk things over with him? When we seek his guidance and blessing?

For most widows, young or old, with children or without, the first major decision is where to live.

If you are an apartment dweller, the answer is usually fairly simple. You remain there. At least until the lease expires. This gives you time to weigh what you really want to do. What you can afford to do.

I was an apartment dweller, but I moved.

About five years before my husband's death, we sold our Chicago home and purchased a vacation and future retirement home in Arkansas. We moved into an apartment.

Shortly after his death, our young daughter told me she planned to marry, but some problems made the date indefinite. I was delighted with the news. (We both had been told the dating was getting serious, so my husband had known of it.) I offered to pay for her wedding providing she kept the cost within a certain amount.

I longed to stay. To be in all the plans. However, a long ingrained habit prevented me. Whenever I have a major decision to make, I not only pray, but I tally up all the advantages and the disadvantages. The answer was plain and clear.

I could drive. Therefore, I could be independent, though our Arkansas home was two miles from a town. (It may be feasible for some of you to learn to drive.)

After paying my rent I would have fifty cents left if I remained in the Chicago area. One pension check would pay the taxes for an entire year in Arkansas. The rent I saved by moving enabled me to pay for our young daughter's wedding without dipping into my savings.

My move proved right for me. I love my new home and area. My neighbors eased my transition and my adjustment both to widowhood and to a small town. My new church brings daily blessings.

If you own a house, make a tally of your own.

Can you afford to maintain it? Are you able to do the work involved? Would an apartment or a condominium or a place with your children, or with your parents, be better?

When a close friend of ours died, his widow was fortunate to have mortgage insurance. The home was hers without any further payments. Still, she knew her son planned to be married. He would be leaving. Should she continue to rattle around in the big house, the house so full of memories? She positively hated apartments. She also disliked yard work. She was employed full time.

My husband suggested she add up the regular expenses, include a logical amount for repairs, etc., and see how much per month it would cost her. He had her figure how much interest she would realize on the money if she sold. When she had these figures she could determine not only the feasibility of keeping her house but how much rent she could afford to pay if she chose to sell. For her the answer proved to be: sell.

Another couple bought their first home late in life. They owned it only seven years when he died. She was over sixty. While she worked she could keep up the payments. She decided to stay.

The home was small and comfortable. She loved digging in the dirt and nurturing the flowers that filled her yard with beauty and fragrance. Though no longer employed, she still lives there. She is now in her late seventies. On occasion she has had a college-age lad and an older woman as roomers and boarders. This keeps her active and ensures that she, herself, has proper food and some companionship. Her flowers are always available to take to a friend, to church for the altar, to a sick person.

Owning a house always involves yard work. My husband was the yard man. Questions flooded my mind, as they may yours. Could I care for a yard? Would help be available?

"Max," my husband once said, "if you can get someone to mow the grass, I don't think you'll have any trouble." But wasps, spiders, snakes? I have survived the year of the mouse, the year of the snake, and the year of the cricket. Now only the beasties out there know what year this will be.

But there are positive aspects to outdoor work. For me nothing can replace the thrill of the birds. Identifying my first yellow-breasted, black-bibbed meadowlark and his wife. Seeing the different personalities of the hummingbirds who drink at my feeder. The other day I discovered a yellow-throated warbler with the distinctive white markings on the side of his head.

The purple finch and goldfinch visit. The mockingbird does trampoline work on my telephone pole, singing all the while. At dusk I hear the whippoorwill and Bob White. Occasionally I detect the soft cooing of the mourning dove. These are different birds from the ones I watched at my Chicago feeder. There I enjoyed most the bright, happy cardinals. They make me feel at home because they come for my sunflower seeds here, too. How grateful I am that God created the birds for us to enjoy!

One Sunday my neighbor told me I had bagworms on

one of my globe arborvitae. I must get them off and burn
them, she said, or they would destroy the bush. The next
morning I went out and solemnly apologized to the bush
for what I was about to do. Then I clipped off every branch
with a bagworm. I burned it all.

That afternoon I told my neighbor how moth-eaten my
bush looked. "Moth-eaten?" she asked. "Why should it
look moth-eaten?"

I told her what I had done. It seems I was not supposed
to have clipped off the branches. I should have just pulled
off the bags. Sometimes I need a detailed road map to
follow. She forgot to give me the directions for the cutoff.

I cut out "how to" articles from my husband's *Popular
Mechanics*. I've screwed my first screw and nailed my
first nail. I'll admit I'm not very good at any of these
things. But let's face it. All of us are greenhorns in some
way.

If you, too, decide to move, perhaps your friends will
place you in categories, as mine did. Some thought me
very courageous to go alone to a new place, to people I
only slightly knew. They didn't realize that I'm really a
little stupid. I don't usually expect any problems.
Sometimes I don't have any.

Others declared me foolish. "You're moving to an area
where everyone is older than you are," some said.
Whether they said so or not, they thought I was silly to
move because I was young enough to marry again and
would have more opportunity in Chicago.

Perhaps they didn't realize the ratio of widows and

divorcees and single women to available men. It's pretty
scary if you plan on remarrying.

When they voiced the "foolish" opinion, I'd reply, "If it
took me nearly forty years to find a man who could 'turn
me on' I'll probably never find another in this life." I'm
living alone, in my own house, and I'm content.

Living alone may be right for you, too, or you may wish
to live with one of your children.

Ann Landers recently said the answers to whether
couples were glad or sorry they had children were running
70 percent in favor of not having had them. This is a sad
commentary on both parents and children. However, if
you have them, they may want you to live with them. Pray
and listen and wait a long time before making a final
decision.

A widow I know made this choice and is very happy. She
didn't know how to drive. Her neighborhood was old and
decaying. Crime was increasing. Now she relaxes in her
own sitting room, bedroom, and bath. Her daughter and
son-in-law work. There are no grandchildren. She helps
with many things around the house. She can join her
children and their friends when she pleases or retire to her
own TV, her books, her handwork. She is a very lucky
woman.

Another widow moves from place to place. Her
daughter-in-law will no longer have her. One daughter is
married to a serviceman, and sometimes they must move
to climates too hot or too cold for the mother's comfort.
One daughter has too many youngsters. Another sometimes speaks abruptly and talks back. The one who was

the best daughter—in the widow's opinion—is now dead. Living with her children has not been the happiest solution for her.

Some of you are young widows. You may also face the question of where to live. Here, once again, take God into your plans and get busy with a tally sheet. Also, necessity may guide your decision.

I sang for the wedding of a beautiful girl. She and her husband were happy, became the parents of one child and expected another. Life looked bright and beautiful when a tragic accident changed it completely.

Unable to work until after the baby's birth, the young widow originally thought to leave her apartment and move back to her parents. Considering the idea, she then rejected it and made a down payment on a condominium with some of her insurance money. There are others her age about, and other children. No yard work or such. She says it's the best decision she has made.

Another young woman, mother of five, was grief stricken when her husband, inexplicably, took his life. Support for her family was necessary. She lived in a suburban area. She knew she couldn't take her five children to her parents. Besides, they lived in another state, in a town where public transportation was nonexistent. This widow didn't drive, so she sold her suburban home and bought a smaller one in the city.

If you don't drive, like the widow just mentioned, you may be forced to move to another location, where mass transportation is available. Or you could consider learning to drive.

Driving is a skill. It is not easy for everyone, but knowing how is advantageous and sometimes necessary.

I know several widows who have sold the cars that only their husbands drove. Some have moved when, if they had known how to drive, they could have remained.

One of my neighbors lost her husband two years ago. She is one of the youngest "75s" I've ever met. Several of us would, and do, drive her on errands. However, she has learned to drive. She rarely does, but she knows how.

Recently, she figured it costs an average of $28.00 a month for her to keep her car. If she adds her initial investment, the possible interest on that investment, and the maintenance figure, her average monthly cost is nearer $45.00. Her husband once told her a car costs $3.65 a day. Before he died he suggested she sell it and use a taxi. She is still debating the issue in her mind.

Like her, you must ask the questions, Is it worth it? Is it necessary? Do I want to make changes? Learn a new skill?

Perhaps, if you are near her age, you might consider entering a retirement home. There are many good ones. Some church-affiliated complexes are worth every penny you pay.

A widowed friend of our family entered one about sixteen years ago. Her next birthday will be her ninety-fourth. She's undergone cataract surgery, several infirmary stays, and everything she has needed has been supplied. Her room is lovely. The food is tasty and well balanced.

A home removes the fear of ever being dependent upon your children, relatives, or friends. In many, there is freedom to go and come, to vacation with friends and relatives; and the personnel may arrange jaunts of one kind or another for the residents.

Like the other choices, this should be approached with a prayer for guidance and with careful thought and wise choosing. One widow chose a lovely place, but it is over fifty miles from those she knows. Many of her old friends are widows like herself and do not drive. There is no public transportation. She is a lonely woman.

Sometimes loneliness comes when least expected. A recently widowed friend sat in my living room the other day, along with one of her married sons and a daughter, both of whom live over five hundred miles from us. The widow had lived here for some years with her husband. He had been a partial invalid, so she became accustomed to driving, yard work, and so forth.

I told Ted and Mary I hoped they wouldn't mind if I gave their mother some advice about moving. My advice was for her to remain here with her friends rather than move close to her children. Children, like friends, lead busy lives. They are involved in their own interests. There are times when living in close proximity to your children brings not only loneliness but frustration. Parents discover the young people don't have much time for them.

"I know. We thought Mary should call us more often," Mrs. B. laughingly said, looking at her daughter.

"Well, Mom, now that you've spent more time at my house you know how busy I'm kept with my five," her daughter replied.

Think carefully before pulling up stakes. Don't ask for frustration as well as loneliness.

Occasionally this works in reverse. The mother of one of my daughter's friends is deliberately smothering her only child, a daughter. The girl has been married two years. Every morning about eleven she goes to her daughter's home. "The house is lonely," she mentions. As bedtime approaches she says, "OK, get your pajamas." The widow expects her daughter to come and sleep at the widow's home.

At first the daughter was sympathetic. Now she knows it is putting a strain on her marriage. And it's not helping her mother adjust. In addition to this, I heard the mother is planning to move in with the young couple. She hasn't even asked their opinion. Think of your sorrow, yes, but don't let it turn you into a selfish, demanding, self-pitying individual.

The place you live can be beautiful. Even if you live alone. Wherever you live, remember the apostle Paul. He was content in whatever place he found himself.

Many people take the verse out of the context and say, "Money is the root of all evil." The Bible says, "The *love* of money is the root of all evil."

Tragedy is sad, no matter what income level you are on. However, it's easier to be sick or unhappy *with* money than without it. After the tumult and the shouting die, you need to reassess your finances.

My husband and I each invested a small amount of money in mutual funds. For some years he moaned about how low they'd fallen. "Max," he'd say, "if they'd only go back to where we bought them, I'd sell." He held on, hoping for a miracle.

Many women are at a loss when a major decision about money has to be made. Before my marriage I was independent in many ways. In fact, it was one of the complaints my boyfriends uttered. My mother and I discussed things after my father died, but I had the final word. It was hard to convince myself I'd become so dependent in marriage. I knew one of my first decisions should concern those mutual funds.

From time to time I scanned the investor's page. I remembered an article that counseled checking with two brokers. If they agreed, your course was set. Then you were to pick the broker who appealed to you personally, the one with whom you felt more rapport. I'm chicken at heart, I guess. My brokers agreed with each other. I liked them both. So I took some advice from each.

I sold the mutual funds eight months before the S.E.C. stopped trading, when the price fell from twenty dollars to ten cents in five years. I lost money, but not as much as I would have if I had procrastinated.

There's no shame in making a mistake. We all do. It's only harder to bear when money is involved.

So what can you do? How can you make your money work more efficiently for you? In spring, 1976, *Glamour* magazine held twenty More for Your Money workshops across the country. Similar sessions, giving financial management tips, are sure to be offered by others in the future.

Recently my bank sent out a beautifully designed flyer

about a new type of checking account—one that allows you to do an amazing number of things for a minimum amount per month. When I read it carefully, I discovered my personal use would be limited to about five hundred dollars' worth of traveler's checks. Under the advertised system, I'd pay out more than twice as much as those checks normally cost me.

Shop around for your checking account. Some institutions specify age brackets in which you pay only for the printing of the checks. Some have no minimum-balance requirement, thus enabling you to realize some interest on the money you might otherwise have to keep in your checking account.

Savings accounts vary in interest. Of course, you need a rainy-day account where money is easily accessible. Your interest will not be high. For many of you it is best to look around, asking, Where can I obtain the most for my investment in an insured savings institution?

When a loan is necessary for a car, an improvement on your home, medical expenses, or an emergency, investigate several avenues. If you have access to a company credit union, you may find this is the cheapest. I have always borrowed vacation money from my company credit union. My share account with them is not touched. My loan is insured. When I safely return, I transfer the money from my savings to my loan.

Most of us women "comparison shop." We read the food ads, the apparel ads. Use this same investigative procedure in other financial matters. Snap up and snoop out the best buy for your needs.

And don't eliminate the possibilities your church offers. Our singing youth group finances a "work and concert" trip every summer. One year they taught daily vacation Bible school in Jamaica. Another year they renovated the chapel on an Indian reservation in Oklahoma. Last year they planned and chopped out hiking trails in a newly established, interdenominational Bible camp in Kentucky. They eagerly search for jobs. I've put in my order. I want a yard man to dig out some roots and rocks, to help me clean out and plant creeping phlox in a problem area.

So read financial columns, attend money lectures, take courses in finance management, and ask questions. Comparison shop, and you'll be pleased and surprised with the results.

The delightful part of this search is that it helps both the moneyed and those of us who must be frugal. Sometimes frugality necessitates making a decision about looking for work or continuing at your usual job. Here, too, give full thought to your decision. Most of us lose our mate at a time when freedom of choice is available. Children are grown, or nearly so. Parents may be gone. Therefore, money is no longer the greatest incentive in a job. Satisfaction and happiness in what you are doing may be more important factors.

Because of home responsibilities, before my marriage I always had to have a job in one hand before I let go with the other. However, when I felt too unhappy, too bored, or in need of a job with more challenge and chance of advancement, I prayed and looked and moved.

My young widowed friend whose husband died while she

was expecting their second child, needed income. One of her jobs was addressing envelopes at home. It allowed her to work when she wished and still provide care for her small children. After she moved into her condominium, she worked for the construction company that had built it. She greeted prospective buyers and showed the models.

The widow who was left with five young boys found a job as a waitress after she moved into the city.

It is possible to find the right position for your specific need. Use my method—pray.

Before my marriage, as I mentioned, I prayed. I could relate at least seven stories of how God led me to different jobs or to better positions within the same company. I'll only mention one—the one that led, a year later, to my meeting my husband.

The position I held was challenging, interesting, and nerve-wracking. Promotions were not fairly distributed. One girl, with one and one half years of service, was promoted over many who had ten times as much experience and time with the company. The office was in an uproar. Especially when the company assigned her back to our office. Then, unhappy, she asked for a demotion back to our level six months later. This wasn't bad enough. Three months later she was again promoted. (Her father knew many of the company officers.)

Shortly after this, our new manager interviewed each of us. We were told our strong points and our weaknesses. We were to tell him our gripes. I did.

I'd been praying about the inequity. So I explained

quietly and unemotionally how I felt. He mentioned the one promotion he'd been privy to.

"Dorothy deserves it," I said. "But for every Dorothy, there are five Marges."

"Can you name some others?" he asked.

I did. As well as the reasons for their promotions.

Four months later he arranged for me to work on a special project. A project that resulted not only in a promotion but in my ultimately meeting the greatest guy I'll ever know.

What God has done for me, he can do for you. He is no respecter of persons. He knows our needs. He helps us in all our decisions. Even the ones we wish did not confront us.

During my husband's illness I chose to take my pension even though my boss suggested a leave. I forfeited 6 percent per year for each year I was under fifty-five. My husband died exactly one month after my pension was effective.

I could have returned to my old job, my pension rescinded, and I could have received a lucrative salary again. However, I chose to remain retired to follow my dream—my dream to write.

Of course I have to budget. Sometimes my checkbook reads only $2.35. But I'm happy. I'm doing what I want to do. You can, too. So what if the money is scarce? It isn't suffering when you are doing what you really want to do. It isn't deprivation. God promises to supply all our needs. Not necessarily our wants but all—*all*—our needs.

The freedom of widowhood may enable you to get a job

you've always dreamed of. Most of us, doing what we like,
find it never a chore, money no real object. You, like me,
are now free to choose. Choose wisely.

One of my friends—a very capable, fast, accurate
worker—has always commanded top wages. She is now a
widow. At present she has been transferred to a
department she hates. Her boss is difficult to work with.
The job demands things she has always despised doing.
The money is very good.

She stays because she is now in her mid-fifties. Her age
is a detriment, she thinks. She has a physical condition—
under control, but a possible hindrance to employment
elsewhere. She has a chance of a pension if she works
another six years, and probably no chance of a pension at a
new place.

I'm human, so I gave her advice. She's a Christian, so
she should lay it on the line to God.

No job is worth being as unhappy about as she is.
Unhappiness undermines your looks, your temperament,
your health. It's not worth it mentally or physically, I told
her. The frustrations, hatreds, and resentments engen-
dered by her job seem a worse fate to me than trying, with
God's help, to get another employer to overlook her real or
imagined disabilities.

What about the possible pension? My philosophy is the
kind depicted by the "fruit in my lunch" story. One day I
did not bring any fruit with my lunch.

"Max," a friend said. "How come no fruit?"

"Well, we had one pear last night. I was hungry. I
decided I might not be alive today so I ate it."

My friend has, apparently, made her decision. Her conversation is liberally sprinkled with all the problems related to her job. She's gaining weight, possibly indicating her unhappiness. She is often exhausted.

Save and plan for a rainy day, but don't forget to live today. Tomorrow doesn't always appear.

A pension is worth having. I'm glad I receive a small one. But God answers prayer. He knows *all* our needs. He promises to supply. To lead us. We will not always be happy, but we can be relaxed and at peace with ourselves and our fellow men.

When making your decisions, line up the facts; list the advantages and the disadvantages. Be honest. Pray. Then, with God on your side, join me and say, "I am not afraid to face tomorrow, for I have seen yesterday and I love today."

5

God's Great Goodness – Friends

Suddenly—no calls, no invitations, nothing!

This probably has happened or will happen to you. It has to every widow and widower I know.

Don't fret. If it's any consolation, it happens when parents die, when children die, and so on. It's a fact of life and is in no way related to how much you are liked or thought about by others.

Friends are wonderful. When tragedy strikes, they are always there. Many of them know exactly what to do for you. Sometimes it's just to be present—strong, solid, and silent. After a death they often throw open their homes to you, invite you out for dinner, and drop in on you.

Then—suddenly—little or nothing.

Try hard not to feel bad when this happens. Don't get bitter. Don't deride them. They have just become caught up again in their own affairs. They haven't forgotten you. But they think the critical time, the horrible part of the shock, should be over. Accept this.

Or do as one woman does. Whenever she is lonely or sad she gets into her car and drives. Midnight or otherwise. She rediscovers the mysterious beauty of the night or the color of God's world. The serenity of the countryside casts its peace on her life, and she returns thanking God.

Don't be overly distressed by the forgetfulness of friends, for now is the time you really start your new life.

Some couples who have been friends will completely sever their relationship with you. You are no longer a couple. You are the oddball, the fifth wheel. They do not realize that someday they may be in your place. Or perhaps they sense this and do not wish to be reminded. Continue to do your part, but do not force these friendships.

My husband and I enjoyed a wonderful relationship with a couple. We'd traveled together. Visited often. After my husband died I made three calls to them in the four months I remained in the Chicago area. They called me once and wrote me one letter after my move.

I miss them. I really do. But in their place have sprung up others. Friends, couples, not as intimate before but now proving wonderful, every step of this lonely way.

This will happen to you.

Most of your friends will continue to make life as pleasant as they can. They will remain true.

However, friends can only do so much. They encourage you. They suggest ideas to challenge your abilities and fill your empty hours. They try to get you interested in some "alone things." But, if you refuse to try any of these and want only to be on the receiving end for invitations out, if you sit before the television and hug your grief about you like a robe—in other words, if you *refuse* to recover—then your friends may envision slipping away to more receptive individuals.

You are the only one who can lick this thing. You and God.

My husband lost his first wife in a tragic auto accident. He knew what it meant. He counseled others, telling them that friends are wonderful.

"However," he'd say, "most of this adjustment must be made by you alone. From inside. From resources you've built up through the years. Friends, much as they might like to do so, cannot do it all."

Some people have more inner resources than others. Some have more determination. Some rise more readily to challenges. Some put more trust in God. But, if you are lonely, if you are unhappy, if you can't seem to shake your "widow blues," don't blame your friends. Take a look at yourself.

A friend of mine was blessed with understanding and never-give-up friends. For two years she was bitter, critical, unhappy, dissatisfied. If a chum called, it was not unusual to be greeted with, "It's about time you telephoned."

This turned off some, but not the tried and true. We loved her. We believed in her. We knew that one day she would wake up to life.

Finally she came through. Not all the way at first, but she took stock of herself. Knew *she* had to do something. Her first step was to join a group dedicated to weight loss. As the pounds began to drop off, her smile returned. Her enjoyment of life and friends increased. She was happier because she had started on the road back. In her new satisfaction with herself, she even returned to her former mode of service in the church.

Don't let it take you as long as it took her. Don't wait two years to begin. Begin today.

An Ann Landers column once carried a letter from a widow incensed at receiving letters addressed "Mrs. *Mary* Smith" instead of "Mrs. *John* Smith." Ann Landers told her she was right. She should be addressed as "Mrs. *John* Smith."

I, too, am proud that I am still Mrs. Clifford Jensen. But, if a friend takes time out from her busy day to write me a letter, I don't care how she addresses it. I'll never waste time quibbling about it. I'll thank her and love her and look forward to her next epistle. It's the letter, the thought, the time consumed that is important.

Remember all your old friends, far and near. Keep those ties but seek out new ones. If you belong to a church, lodge, or any kind of group, there must be one person who appeals to you. Someone you never had time to cultivate before.

Extend an invitation—to shop, to a play or movie, to a museum, to church. Others may be lonely, too. They may be shy.

Basically, people don't change a great deal as they grow older. The shy ones usually remain that way. Throughout my life I've discovered people that others passed by. Mainly they've been the ones who came regularly to church but never spoke to anyone. I like people. I talk to everyone. So . . . I begin gabbing. Soon I discover they are only shy. And they find out I care.

Do you care? Enough to look away from yourself and seek out someone who may also be shy? Someone who is longing to have a best friend just like you? Why not try this search? Find a new friend. Today!

6

So You Think You Have Problems?

Last night I was awake until after 3:00 A.M. Not because I've become a swinger in my widowhood but because, like many widows, I suffer one of their most common complaints. Sometimes I can't sleep.

When this happens to you, remember three important facts:

1. Sleeplessness is not limited to widows and widowers.
2. There is something you can do about it.
3. It, too, will pass.

Advertisements bombarding us from every direction prove we are not alone. Talk to friends. Accidentally eavesdrop. The fact will be confirmed.

The knowledge that we are not alone, however, doesn't make it easier. We fuss. We fume. We try to do something about it. Especially if we hold a full-time job. Our looks and our physical well-being may be undermined. And fear of the results of this increase the pressure within.

When one is retired, or if he or she has sufficient funds so that working outside the home is not essential, the problem exists, but there is no pressing need for an immediate solution. Many enjoy short naps taken anytime.

Whether we work for a living or not, the same things can help.

Just last night one of my recently widowed friends told me she hates to imagine what would have happened to her if the doctor had not prescribed an excellent relaxant drug when Phil died. Not that it is regularly necessary now, but the bottle stands on the shelf. It's there. Its presence comforts her.

This route is the easiest. It will enable you to surmount your immediate problem. Yet, it may eventually be the hardest method. An older woman still relies on such a drug eight years after the initial need. Use this method if you choose, but remember that the Bible says to "let your moderation be known unto all."

It also tells us God gives his beloved sleep. It reminds us that we can lie down in peace and sleep, for he makes us dwell in safety. Sometimes, as Catherine Marshall has found out through experience, he has a reason for our sleeplessness.

God created us to love life. To be aware. To savor things to the full. And some of us don't want anything to dull the emotions that run the gamut of our soul, bitter though they may be.

When you like to sleep, you don't enjoy sleeplessness. When you've always slept well, sudden, sad wakefulness becomes a new, strange, and very unpleasant problem.

Try always going to bed at a regular hour. Sometimes this works. Or go to bed when you are tired. Nine forty-five one night, midnight the next.

Consciously try to relax every muscle. Relaxing the tongue is said to induce sleep. I tried it. Perhaps I didn't know how to do it, because it didn't work for me. But try it. As the old saw says, nothing ventured, nothing gained.

Some people find reading a slumber producer. Others may become too interested and end up reading the book from cover to cover.

Several things seem to aid me. My best procedure is to climb into bed the tired way. If this fails, I relive our trip to the World's Fair in Seattle. For some queer reason, I'm impelled to start the trip at Old Faithful. I rarely get beyond the steep wagon tracks we were forced to travel on the way down from the cemetery at Lead.

Or I pray more earnestly for the problems of my friends. Mine seem to grow dimmer in the process.

Often, if you are not asleep within an hour, it pays to get up. Pick up a piece of handwork. Go to the bathroom. Walk out into the kitchen. Fix a cup of tea. Drink a glass of milk. Or take an aspirin with the milk. See if God has a message for you by scanning his Word.

Even if you must get up for work the following morning, these things may help you. I was forced to apply these "busy" measures while my husband was still on his feet and I was employed. Love, dread, and concern often walked with me as unshakable companions.

Act as though it doesn't matter whether you drop off at 9:30 P.M. or 4:00 A.M. So you can't slip into relaxing, restorative rest. Tomorrow you will probably sleep like a baby.

Sleep eludes most of us when decisions and thoughts

press in. If the thoughts are sad, try to think of lovely times.

The crisis night in my widowhood, the night when I remembered, I tried everything. Still I cried constantly from 11:00 P.M. until 4:30 A.M. I could not force that October picture to fade. That remembrance of my husband taking his last look at autumn. At the beauty of God's world. Even now, as I write, tears are coursing down my cheeks. Finally, I got up. I began to write. I could scarcely see. The page shriveled under my falling tears.

I often think of times like that. Then I try to recall the twinkle growing in his eye when he planned to tease. Or the time I grabbed his hand and dragged him into the kitchen to see the beauty of my walleyed pike baking in the oven, tomato slices peeking out from the middle and on the top, partially covered by golden brown crumbs. I wanted to share that picture. He never ceased to be amazed at the childlike delight I displayed over very simple things.

So remember. Remember the good times. Sleep will come.

The decisions that sometimes cause sleeplessness exhaust you. One of my worst days began with a moving estimator calling. He wanted to arrive earlier. Then another estimator telephoned, desiring to come later. Would they meet?

That same day I had to collect my income-tax records. The tax consultant was to arrive that night.

I was busy writing checks for the renewal of my driver's license, my house insurance, my life insurance, and so on.

I had to get these nuisance things out of the way. I was planning a trip to Spain and a visit with our oldest daughter before my move out of state.

By the way, if you drive and plan to move out of state, check the renewal date of your license. I made a mistake in this. You may profit from my experience. Since my license expired in April and I was leaving the last week in March for my trip to Spain, I sent in my renewal in March. I returned the middle of April, and my three-year Illinois license was waiting for me. When I applied for one in Arkansas at the beginning of May, I was told I would have to pay the full charge for a two-year period. I wrote the proper party in Illinois, explained the circumstances, and asked for a refund. My reply was no, and it was a form letter.

Again I wrote. I stated I didn't know if I'd be happy in Arkansas, and didn't wish to pay five years of charges to realize only two years of use. Once more a letter came with a no. However, in their magnanimous way, they said if I returned to Illinois within the three-year period they would reinstate my license at no charge—*"providing you return to the same address."* Big deal! So, if you are moving out of state, inquire about a temporary license. Don't spend money needlessly, as I did.

Finally, that night, after one of my worst days, I dropped into my big chair. Had I done the right thing? Should I try to move? Should I have retired—or rather remained so? With all my heart I wished I had a brother or an uncle or someone who really loved me to counsel me. For a moment I forgot my most precious, my most concerned friend—God. God, who knows our every need before we ask.

I started to read the newspaper. I always read back to front. Probably habit from the days when the funnies were on the back page. I noticed the investor's column.

As I read I thought, "This sounds like I wrote it—but I didn't." The case was almost parallel to mine. The age, place of employment, length of service, benefits, and desires were almost identical. The correspondent wondered whether he was crazy to want to retire and try to write. It would be a new career. With inflation, financial benefits, and so on, friends told him he'd be out of his mind to do so. But he felt if he wanted to write he must begin before he became any older. What should he do?

The answer was my answer. As if from God, himself. "I won't snow you that life will be a bed of roses," the column started. It closed with, "I think you're going to have a ball."

What an ending to my otherwise completely frustrating day! With tears in my eyes, I thanked God.

Last—in all good time—this, too, will pass.

Often lonesome, but never lonely. Does this describe you? There is a difference between them, you know.

To lose a parent, a child, a friend is always hard. The void looms before you.

Severing connections with a life partner creates more than a void. It is a Grand Canyon. You'll feel for a long time as though you are traveling down ever deeper into a great yawning abyss. You're on the back of an indecisive, slow-footed donkey. Suddenly, you'll realize you are on your way up—on a sure-footed mule.

Most of the time, women lose their mates after the children are gone. The house is empty. It echoes your footsteps.

You see the ghost of him standing at the bathroom mirror, parting his hair in the middle. "Ten on one side, and eleven on the other," he'd say as he laughed.

You hear the saw in the basement as he works on his newest project. You see him on his first riding mower, grinning like a kid, savoring every moment. Just as he did when he led the Lilac Festival parade astride that big beautiful chestnut. You hear him slamming the left front car door, time after time, seeking to find that squeak.

You hear the music, but there's no one there.

The days pass relatively quickly. The nights are endless. You miss man talk.

Because my husband tragically and suddenly lost his first wife, he liked to be near me. If I was in the basement washing and ironing, he was there busy on one of his projects. If I was in the yard, he washed the car. Naturally I miss this. I liked it.

I'd look up and see him, his head bent, intent on what he was making. The vibrations emitted were very real to me. My heart seemed to swell with love and thankfulness that I was privileged to be his wife. That he had picked me instead of some younger, swinging chick.

I'd stop what I was doing, run over, kiss him on his sweaty neck or sunburned forehead. Impromptu. Spontaneous. But he loved it. He'd look up and appear to burst into life, his eyes sparkling, his smile warm.

I married him because, though I'd gone with very fine boys and men before, he was the first one I'd met I not only loved but felt I could not live *without*. I'd always said this would be the criterion of marriage for me.

"You would have married Cliff," one of my friends used to say, "if he'd had long hair, bare feet, and no job." She's right, you know. He was the one man who turned me on.

However, now I find it's possible to live without him. It isn't easy, that's true. But you, too, can discover you can be lonesome—"having a lonely feeling"—without being lonely—"isolated, longing for friends." I can be alone without feeling forsaken. And you can, too.

When I was young we sang a chorus that went: "No never alone, No never alone. He's promised never to leave me. Never to leave me alone." Jesus keeps his promises.

Fear is very real. More so to one who is alone. It can be soul-consuming, calmly accepted, or actively faced.

A widow I know lives in a lovely "castle." Like those stone fortresses of old, it has various devices and booby traps to keep intruders out. She needs precautions. She lives in an exclusive area in a city with a high murder rate. Her home has been burglarized three times. In these three instances, most of her prized possessions have been taken, but the next criminal doesn't know this. For spite, the next one could horribly mutilate and destroy the home or her.

For many of us, fear is being out late at night on a

shadowy street or entering an empty house. One week when my husband and young daughter were out of town, I locked the door leading to the upstairs and the one leading to the basement every night.

Once when I was very young, my father dead, my mother in the hospital, and our pinchpenny landlord wouldn't fix the broken lock on the downstairs door or the loose hinge on the upper door, I would push a chair under the doorknob. Then I'd go to bed and pray, "Lord, I took care of myself all day, it's up to you tonight." Kid stuff. But being afraid is too real.

When you're unhappy or scared, try to change things. Consider moving to a safer place. There are still some places where you do not have to lock your door. Where packages in an unlocked car are unmolested. Nice places.

If moving is not possible, take precautions. My husband suggested his cousin install doors and an automatic door opener on her garage. "But no one has garage doors here," she said. Later she took his advice. Now, cruising along her street, one cannot tell from a casual glance down her tree-shaded drive whether she is at home.

Look in the back seat before entering your car. It's a favorite hiding place for criminals. Even Barnaby Jones, a television private eye, has been caught on that one.

Have special dead-bolt locks put on your doors. True, if someone really wants to break in, he will. But make it as hard as possible.

Ring the doorbell when entering an empty house or apartment. Most burglars would rather get out than face someone. In ringing the doorbell, you give them a chance.

Never enter when the house appears to have been invaded. Instead, go to a neighbor's and call the police.

Automatic timers are easily connected to the lights to emulate your most regular times and habits. However, don't install an on-at-dusk, off-at-dawn light within your home. A light that burns all night every night is an open invitation to an intruder.

No matter where you live, it's wise to draw your drapes or blinds in the room you are occupying. You never can be sure who's out there looking in. Let them do their peeping at somebody else.

Be alert when out. Avoid shadows. Walk briskly, and away from buildings. A boyfriend once told my mother she needn't worry about me. "She walks so fast and purposefully that a fellow knows she has a destination," he said. These tips may not deter the criminal of today. Nevertheless, they are worth trying.

Do these seem like trite, oft-repeated warnings? They are. However, the observance of them may save your dwelling place and you.

I'm a coward. Especially in an electrical storm. One night, as I watched TV, one descended. Suddenly. Furiously.

My husband always laughed when I wanted to pull out the plug on the set. So I stoically and miserably determined not to do so that night.

When I finally flipped the switch, the clap of thunder in the sudden stillness engulfed me. I started to shake. I moved unsteadily down the hall. Just as I reached the bedroom, the lightning lit it up like day. The rain on my porch canopy sounded like bullets.

Quickly I undressed. Hurriedly I got into bed. I pulled the pillow over my head, crouching in a small, isolated ball, trembling. My breath unsteady and much too quick. No strong, solid body beside me. No arms to enfold me.

Then, mentally, I shook myself. "Nothing you can do will stop the fury of the storm," I thought. "Only God calmed the sea. He can calm you. He can keep you—and your house—as safe as he wants you to be."

Slowly I stretched out my legs. I put the pillow *under* my head. I stopped shivering.

The storm continued. It was the same storm, of the same intensity. But I rested in a safe harbor. I was in the hollow of God's hand.

When we have grown accustomed to having someone beside us we may fear not only storms but also going into a restaurant or on a trip alone. Sometimes we forego these pleasures.

I looked with mingled fear and anticipation toward visiting our daughter in Spain. It would be my first big trip alone. It was to a foreign country, in whose language only some polite phrases, counting to ten, and the word for milk were included in my vocabulary.

I dreaded changing planes in New York. For me, anticipation is often as real as the actual occurrence. It can be heaven or hell.

So I prayed.

I was one of the first to alight from the Chicago plane. By chance or by God's design, I overheard a man asking about the same flight I sought. I followed him. I was the fourth person signed in.

The waiting room was extremely large, the furniture enormous and of black leather. As I sat down I sank much deeper than I'd anticipated. Clutching the arms of the chair, I struggled to extricate myself.

The black sofas; the smoke-tinted windows with the darkness of night closing in; the high, vaulted ceiling; and the ticket counter line stretching down an endless tube of light made me feel infinitesimal.

Tears suddenly sprang to my eyes. We had intended to take this trip together. Now I was alone. And he—he would never see his grandchildren again in this life. Once he had remarked we were luckier than our daughter's in-laws. "They're older, Max," he said. "They'll probably never live to see the children become adults."

I'd seldom felt so alone as in this cavernous room, buried in this deep, black, coffin of a chair, the darkness pressing in upon me.

Then suddenly I noticed the other passengers streaming in. Clothes bags! Tote bags! Camera bags! Golf bags! I couldn't believe it. If they were carrying this much on board, what had they put in the baggage compartment?

I began to laugh through my tears. I must have been an oddity, with only my purse and a paperback book. I knew now why I was one of the first to alight from the other plane.

Before leaving home I determined I would try to look as though I knew exactly where I was going. That I would walk purposefully. Therefore, in the Madrid airport, it was really not a surprise when a girl about twenty approached me.

"Can you tell me how to get to customs?" she asked.

"I don't know exactly," I laughed. "But come with me. We'll find it together."

I must have looked so sure of myself that I even eluded my son-in-law. "How did you get past me?" he said when he discovered me calmly waiting by the door leading to the parking lot.

How you walk, how you hold your head, can give an impression of inner calm and confidence.

Once I had a voice teacher who wore the most fantastic hats. Most of us would not have looked twice at them much less put them on top of our heads. But, when she placed one carefully, she stood straight, cocked her head a little to the side, lifted her chin—and that hat was her. On her, such hats belonged. She carried herself as if to say, "Isn't everyone wearing them?"

Most of us are more like a friend of mine who was attracted to a certain shawl but felt silly when she tried it on. I advised her to let it drape down a bit and walk as if it were exactly the right thing to wear. She took it back. She couldn't overcome her What-will-other-people-think? feelings.

Perhaps the biggest fears of a widow concern finances and health. And decisions revolving about the ownership of a house, a car, and how to take care of them.

Apartment-dwelling widows, you can praise God that you do not have these problems in adjusting. For the home owner, there are questions like, When do you paint the trim on the house? What is the best insurance? Who do you call to trim the trees and shrubs? Those problems never existed for you if, like me, you had a husband who was fantastic at do-it-yourself projects.

Since my house is predominantly brick, I never thought of the painted trim—that is, until my new neighbor pointed out the peak was peeling. The original paint was put on when the house was built, in 1969. So, in 1975, I had it repainted. I asked questions. Now I know what to expect. What kind of paint is best.

So ask questions.

A good friend who lost her husband several months before their car insurance was due last year, was confused. She notified the company of the sale of their second car but didn't understand coverages and such. Her confidence in her husband's wisdom was great. She looked up the old policy, compared the new offer, and decided on the same type of coverage.

Establish good relations with a garage you trust. They will tighten things, tell you when your air filter needs changing, come to your aid when the car won't start.

An older neighbor had some yard work done and asked the price for trimming her trees and bushes. She planned to use the same man for the job. Then she thought, "Am I silly? Should I look further?" As a result she checked the ads, secured another estimate, and paid thirty dollars less for a very satisfactory job.

Her advice to you is sound. Check the competition before you make your decision. She also contends this keeps people from taking advantage of you because you are a widow.

When my widowed mother died, my only fear was what I would do if I ever got sick. For over thirty years she had been there.

One night, while on a date with my husband-to-be, I began to suffer a queasy feeling. On my arrival home, Cliff saw to it that I took the antacid I found in the medicine cabinet. After he left, the pain became almost unbearable. I hated to call our doctor before morning, so all night I kept thinking, "I'm so sick, and I'm all alone."

The next day, when I didn't report for work, Cliff called. He scolded me for not calling him. He would have come back. Later, several friends told me I shouldn't have hesitated to call them.

Telephone them? In my case I didn't even think of them. Friends are wonderful. Especially when illness strikes.

One of my friends pureed special foods and fed them, daily, to a widow who was dying of cancer. Another compassionate friend arranged to have a cancer victim driven daily to the hospital for cobalt treatments.

The women's organizations in your church often supply daily sitter services when illness strikes. They prepare good food, clean houses, and do a myriad tasks.

Don't be too proud to ask for help.

But don't impose. One widow was often invited by a couple to share supper with them. Soon she began to expect to be invited at least once a week and was desolate if "forgotten." Be grateful for your friends, but don't take regular help for granted.

The help of others is greatly appreciated. I realize more fully now why my friends supporting their widowed mothers always welcomed an out-of-town visit from Cliff and me.

It was Cliff who noticed that the refrigerator door closed improperly. That the toaster no longer popped up the bread. That the step to the back porch sagged. He didn't just observe these things, he fixed them.

Some problems must be solved by us. By you and me.

One of these problems is how we eat. Many widows (I'm one of them) may love to cook, but find eating alone unpleasant. Therefore, they either "piece" all the time, eat out a lot and grow fat, or they lose, lose, lose.

I admire a woman I know because she always prepares a well-balanced meal for herself. If the weather is nice, she puts a pretty cloth on the little table on her balcony. Sometimes she adds a flower or two in a lovely vase and serves herself as if she were presiding over a large banquet table full of guests. On other days she arranges an attractive tray and eats in front of her TV set.

It isn't difficult to treat yourself to a balanced meal. Freezers or freezer compartments are available to most of us. I prepare stew (minus too many potatoes, which do not freeze well), Swiss steak, and ground meat mixtures. I divide them up into small freezer containers and have the main part of my meal ready. That's the hardest part.

Cookbooks for two are available. Helpful hints appear in newspapers and magazines.

One widow gained thirty-five pounds in the first three months after her husband's death. I, too, have gained. But

I'm looking in the mirror. I wanted to look nice for him. Shouldn't I want to be trim for my own sake?

Above all, put your hand in God's hand. With *all* your fears, *all* your problems. Start out with, "What time I am afraid, I will trust in thee." You will surely progress to "I will trust, and not be afraid."

Press on as if everything is going to be all right. "Perfect love casteth out fear."

7

Free to Choose

Women's lib. What freedom! What doors to open! What a challenge! Yes—even what fun! As a widow, prepare for your own personal liberation.

The disadvantages of no longer traveling as a couple are many. I don't need to enumerate them. You know all the ones I know, and maybe some I haven't found out about yet.

However, the advantages are worth investigating.

Most widows are in the over-fifty age bracket. Perhaps it's the first time in your life you've been granted sufficient time to accomplish what you desire. Enough freedom to pursue it when you want. Assuming, of course, that you have the health and the money and the motivation necessary. This applies not only to grasping knowledge of new things and exploring further depths of talents you already have, but also to old, routine matters. Such as housework.

I'm sure I'm not alone in disliking that task, though I like a clean house. As long as my husband lived and I worked, I scheduled the cleaning. Saturday was the main day. However, on the first of the month I washed the windows on the inside and cleaned the blinds. Every

Tuesday night I tossed an extra load of clothes into the machine and ironed. Every night I toiled over at least one job before I sat down to relax.

Things are different now.

As a young tomboy I vowed never to be a slave to housework. Then my philosophy was, "Don't do anything you dislike if you can hornswoggle another into doing it." As an adult this has been tempered to, "Attempt to obtain a paid worker to do hated tasks."

I still try to clean the blinds once a month. At the same time I put an additive down my septic system and African violet food in my sprinkling can. I don't know about you, but at least a haphazard schedule I need. Without it I'd never succeed with undesirable tasks.

When company leaves, I thoroughly clean the guest room, get it ready for the next occupant, and close the door.

About the time I think the toilet bowls may start to discolor, I completely clean the bathrooms. Lint on the floor signals vacuuming time. The whole house gets it. Spots on a mirror indicate it's time to clean them all. I wipe off my faucets and rub down my shower stall after each use.

Dust is my personal bugaboo. I once told my mother how I despised it. She replied, "Why do you think I always assigned that task to you? I hate it, too."

There's no set pattern in my life for domesticity. As a result, my house is reasonably clean and presentable all the time. The exception? When I'm busy writing. That room is a shambles. Please don't open the door!

Now, housework is kind of fun. It's not the ogre it once was. Many things are now different.

During my thirteen-year marriage I wrote only one article. I sang in the choir but practiced only when I was to sing a solo. My "after a fashion" piano playing faded away. I still seldom practice much, I'm ashamed to say. Perhaps that part of my life has had its day.

I can't know about you, but in the depths of my heart, ever since I can remember, has been the desire to travel. All over this beautiful, God-given world. To drink in the wonders of this planet before I travel to the moon and to rapturous heavenly sights.

My first real opportunity came just after World War II. I'll never forget my first glimpse of majestic, awe-inspiring Niagara Falls. It was there I first realized what God meant by "everlasting covenant." Its sign? A circle. I never knew, until then, a rainbow is round.

Travel during my marriage only whetted my desire for more. An uncle tells me there is one with the wanderlust in each generation of our family. Only one. He was the traveler in his. I am in mine.

Now, once again, as in the old days before Cliff, I shuffle my funds about, deny myself inconsequentials, and save for a trip. As a result, as I write this I'm sitting in the Florida sun, while the Chicago temperature is twenty-six degrees. A chance came for me to drive down with friends. It was unexpected, but I was prepared. Aesop, in "The Ant and the Grasshopper," says, "It is thrifty to prepare today for the wants of tomorrow."

You, too, can do these things. If you must, skimp a little

on the fantastic dessert you really want when out with the girls. Pass up the lovely pant suit you don't need anyway. But you can usually try to do what you really want to do. It's a matter of importance.

As a couple you probably discussed many of your expenditures. Now you can do as you wish.

One wife I know once told me if she wanted something she didn't always get it, but her husband always got what he wanted. Money is plentiful in their household. It should be plentiful in the future. Should she be widowed, she'll have the advantage of being able to buy anything she wants. Most of us are not this fortunate.

Don't waft your money to the four winds, but, if you've always wanted something, save for it. Plan for it. If money is readily available, buy it. Maybe it's a seemingly silly dream of a dollhouse like Colleen Moore's. Perhaps it's an extravagant vision of a full-length mink. It might be a tour of the Holy Land, or of missionary stations in a foreign land. Treat yourself. Plan. Go after what you want.

While I was comparing notes with a friend, widowed last year, we discovered we'd both bought peach weekender suits as our Christmas present to ourselves. Without our husbands to buy us lovely gifts we are treating ourselves. I just purchased a water hose standing rack for my birthday. Isn't that romantic?

What desires have sifted into the background of your life? Have you always wanted to go to college? To ripple your fingers over the keys of an organ? To splash paint on a canvas? To write? Now is the time. You may never be this free again. This is true for the young widow and the working widow as well. Time will cease to seem interminable if you immerse yourself in some creative outlet.

My schedule is a flexible one. I arise when I awaken, exercise, make the bed, and have breakfast. Sometimes I vocalize or practice the piano. Then I sit down to write. Occasionally I scribble until almost suppertime, forgetting lunch. Perhaps the mood will not come, and I merely sit and jot down a note or two, think, watch the cars on the highway, or scrutinize the birds who flit about on my feeder.

Try as I may to regulate handwork and letter-writing, I have no success. The pull of other interests is too great. However, I'm doing what I want most to do. You can, too.

As you may have gathered, I'm not a pusher. The weeds, the dust, the music will all be there tomorrow. I may not. So I live each day God gives me the way it best suits me. The results are happy, contented widowhood. I'm never bored. Always wishing for one more hour in the day. One more hour to enjoy his world. One more hour to do something by his power.

By his generosity, many of us are healthy, productive individuals. And, as such, we have probably donated service and money to various organizations. Now that we have been "liberated," our time is even more available for him.

One dear widow, whose oldest son grew up with me and who has been my "mother confessor," is busy at work for God as she approaches her eightieth year. Her husband never cared much for church. He was a homebody, delighting in visitors but not wanting to be one himself. Not even to visit God's house.

Paul foretold, remember, how marriage sometimes keeps us from worshiping and cleaving to God. This widow, while married, did all she felt possible for the church. Now she rejoices in serving with greater intensity.

Sometimes widowhood releases previously pinched purse strings—not only for material, selfish desires, but for the work of the kingdom of God.

Most of us are left without a legitimate excuse for denying our services and our resources to any project we like. Most of us have no reason for boredom. Most of us can give God the best of our remaining life.

Are you one of the ones who sit home unhappy? If you are, wake up. It could be your own fault. This world overflows with opportunity. Abounds in challenge. Is chock-full of enjoyment. And many things don't cost a cent.

Perhaps you must learn that happiness is a personal thing. Something you, yourself, work at for yourself.

Sometimes happiness is just being needed. Just giving of yourself. Money and health pave the way, but they are not essential to a truly healthy, happy, good life. And I'm sure you know as many living proofs of this as I do.

8

Live Again

It's not too late to live.

You may believe it is. You may be numb enough to feel it is. You may be stupid enough to hope it is. But, believe me—it's not too late to live.

Life is time. Time is the most precious thing we possess.

Sometimes I feel my husband was ready to depart this life because he lived every moment to the full. He rose early in the morning. He didn't want to miss any of the day. If he took a nap, it never lasted longer than ten or fifteen minutes and was sandwiched in on the train between work and home. But only after the paper was read. Perhaps he'd catnap while waiting for something to dry, or just to recoup his energy so he could continue a hard project. He was one of the most active people I ever knew, and it was activity that accomplished something— for us, for others, for God.

Many of you are like he was. Some of you are more like me. I'm a procrastinator. I waste time. When I told my husband I knew we'd view some gorgeous sunrises from our deck in Arkansas, he told me, "When will you ever rise early enough to see them?"

But I have even surprised myself. Now that I don't have

to get up, I do. One day recently I even woke in time to see Soyuz land in Russia. I wanted to wake up, but I didn't set the alarm. Now that I am free of an eight-to-five job, there are so many things to do, a myriad beauties to see, so much knowledge to learn, I can no longer waste time.

Perhaps I feel this way because I've always worked outside the home. Also, it's the first time in my life I've ever had to rely on the alarm clock within me. Finally, I have the freedom to explore, in depth, many of the interests that have drawn me as strongly as the Lorelei drew the Rhine boatmen.

I have found no time to become bitter. Some widows do after the numbness wears off.

They are bitter about the doctor. They are antagonistic toward friends. They are out of love with God. They cease living because of their discontent.

Frequently, widows question God, Why? They feel their prayers for healing or protection were not answered. They do not remember that God *always* answers prayer. Only, his answer may be no.

An Old Testament verse says some of us are removed to save us from what lies ahead. I quoted this to my husband when he told me about his first wife's virulent cancer. Perhaps she was killed in the automobile accident two and a half years after that surgery because they both loved God and worked for him and he wanted to save them from the horrors to come.

I too have questioned why. My husband had worked since he was ten. Often he worked two jobs. He had eagerly looked forward to early retirement and to all the things he hoped to do more of. I too have asked why he was cut off just when that dream appeared to be so close to reality.

My prayer for his *life* was answered, No. My other prayer, for as little misery as possible, for a sane mind, for as easy and as comfortable a death as possible, received an affirmative reply.

There were other blessings. He died the day before our son-in-law was due to fly back to his overseas base (he had been attending a two-week stateside course). He died before the beginning of our coldest and worst week of the winter. It was not necessary for me to try to make daily visits to the hospital over treacherous ice. My ice-experienced son-in-law was available to drive me where I needed to go. Instead of being bitter, I had much for which to thank God.

Are you resentful toward God? Have you turned your back on the church? Reconsider. Recall the ways God helped you. Rejoice in them. Press on in love and faith.

Expect great things. Look forward to these things. Experience them and rejoice. Of my great expectations for this year one has already become a reality. Twelve of my articles have been accepted for publication. My next anticipation involves this book. Soon, I hope, the actuality of a published book by me will stare me in the face. Then, I look forward to being one of the winners in a writers' workshop contest.

Perhaps all three of these will not come to pass. Still, I'm living in anticipation. And, as I've acknowledged before, this, for me, is nearly as much fun as the actuality.

While I'm anticipating these big events, I'm happy with little surprises.

My mother's cousin, a dear lady over eighty, writes to me regularly. Once she wrote that, like my mother, I seemed to receive great delight out of little things. She was glad.

The day I drove through the car wash in town one of those things happened. I decided I would try to wax it myself. It was my first time. Cliff always treated our car to all the TLC. I just drove it.

It was 4:00 P.M. I was invited out for a 6:00 P.M. dinner.

I dutifully read the instructions, smoothed the cream over that lovely automobile, and sat down to wait for the wax to get "thoroughly dry." I relaxed for about ten minutes, then began to polish. As many of you know, I could never begin to complete the job in time.

Sweaty, miserable, at 5:30 I hurriedly drew my second bath of the day. Then, heartsick and defeated, I sped down the highway in a very messy car.

It rained immediately after supper. When I saw the car I almost jumped for joy. The wax might be streaked, but the water stood in big beads on the hood. This was a good sign, my husband always announced.

Another day, I saw a colorful bird and his mate and was able to scan my bird book and discover they were meadowlarks. What an exciting small moment!

Life is made up of many little things. Even the straw that broke the camel's back was a small item. Minute happenings take the humdrum out of life.

One of my widowed neighbors is very self-sufficient.

She has helped me immeasurably. But yesterday, in one of our gully washes, her car conked out. I pointed out that she probably had a flasher signal. I found it and got it working. A little thing, but I was glad I could help her because she's done so much for me.

Seek out and take delight in the little things of life. Remember, God protects even the lowly sparrow. Get excited. Be enthusiastic. Find a cause. It's a great life, and you and I still have time to live.

9

Love Again

It isn't unusual to feel as though you will never love again. Your God. Your family. Your friends. Another man.

There is an emptiness. Vast. Deep. Wide. Impossible ever again to fill.

But you must try.

If you do not, it will be filled. Perhaps with unhealthy thoughts and acts. Remember Matthew 12 and Luke 11 when the cast-out, unclean spirit walked through dry places, seeking rest. Then he returned to his original abode and found the room empty. He entered in and took seven other, more wicked spirits with him. The last state of the man was worse than the first because the vacuum had not been filled with good things. So fill your vacuum. With good things.

First, do not close God out of your life.

Love him. Don't leave him because you think he should have healed your husband. Yes, he could have done so. However, there must have been a good reason that he didn't choose to do so. It's up to you, with his help, to find out what he plans for your future—what is awaiting that only you can accomplish.

God stands right beside you. Closer than your right hand. He stays, hoping you will show some sign you want him as the focal point of your new life. Begin active things to draw yourself closer to him and to conscious knowledge of his great concern for you.

One of these things? Habitually study his Word. Nearly every denomination has a devotional booklet such as *The Upper Room, Daily Bread,* and so on. Some of you may never have practiced daily reading, much less a study of the Bible. If so, these meditation guides will help you begin. Sometimes it will seem uncanny the way the lesson for the day fits you.

Once a widow friend was going through physical difficulties. I wrote her a letter. Though she had never before taken any of the suggestions of her friends, I felt I had to make one more effort.

When she received my letter, I heard her remarks were, "How could Max write me such a letter? I have the best possible surgeon. I pray." And so forth. My heart was sad, but I felt no guilt. I had written that letter after a great deal of prayer. Out of the fullness and the love of my heart for her.

That night the reading for my meditation was Psalm 81. As I read it, I looked up, and said, "God, you know exactly how I feel. It's happened to you, and your decision was the same one I have just made." You will experience these things, too, when you follow a devotional guide.

Should you prefer to read direct from the Bible, you might start with John or Psalms or Proverbs. Or read straight through. If you read two chapters of the Old

Testament and one of the New each day, you should finish the entire Bible in a year. Three chapters is not too much to give God.

Once I imagined the Old Testament was dull reading. I'd plow my way through. And some chapters *were* like that. In others, many others, I found answers to fit my twentieth-century needs. I reaped many benefits.

One night, very disturbed about a matter that was taking a great length of time to resolve, I read, "Why art thou cast down, O my soul? and why art thou disquieted within me? hope thou in God: for I shall yet praise him, who is the health of my countenance, and my God." The next day the ringing telephone brought the beginning of the end of my problem.

Coincidence? Maybe. But I like to believe God spoke to my soul, quieted it down, gave it hope, and then produced for me the chance to praise him.

Another time "Sanctify yourselves: for tomorrow the Lord will do wonders among you," titillated my curiosity. I searched for the meaning of "sanctify" looking up other verses including the word. Then I sought to "sanctify" myself. Our gracious God made the year following one of the best of my life.

You may never progress to investigating Scriptures in the manner in which I looked up sanctification. Perhaps you don't yet desire to make time to attend study courses at your church, at a Christian school, or through correspondence. Don't feel guilty about this as long as you make it a daily habit to read some portion of God's Word. He will honor that. Sooner or later, as you grow in him, he will lead you into a deeper, richer study of his marvelous message.

Start a daily prayer time if you've never had one before. Begin by requesting wisdom and understanding as you read the Bible. God will reveal himself and his will for you.

The marvelous thing about prayer is that it's available to you anytime, anywhere. He hears. He answers. You can pour out your needs, your sorrows, your hurt to him kneeling beside your bed. You can launch a rocket for help as you walk along a strange shadowy street, or encounter a tantalizing temptation.

One time I was frightened by footsteps behind me. I was in unfamiliar territory at dusk. I beamed a prayer aloft.

It seemed as though Someone said, "Turn around." When I swung backward, there was a man not five feet behind me, arms outstretched to grab me. I opened my mouth to scream. Though I'd hit high F above high C at my voice lesson a few minutes before, nothing came. The man darted back to the alleyway and out of my sight. In an emergency, it doesn't take God long to answer.

As you read, as you pray, his promises will weave an undergirding hammock for your soul. You'll never forget his Words. "I will never leave thee, nor forsake thee." "My God shall supply all your need." "All things work together for good to them that love God."

And last, don't forsake church services. Don't be like one widow I know who goes only a couple of times a year. Then she becomes upset because she arrives on the Sunday of the conference report or on student recognition day. If she attended more frequently, she would obtain more food for her soul.

So make church attendance another habit.

Death sometimes makes families act queerly. Makes loving them difficult.

It usually isn't the death itself. It's the money or diamonds or other material things that twists them in various ways.

A certain mother-in-law wanted her diamonds to go to her daughter-in-law. The girl knew of the desire, but she and her husband were miles away when his mother died. The mother's sister-in-law also knew of the bequest. When she and the widow's brother cleaned out the home, she took all the diamonds. She planned to give the young girl the wedding and engagement rings, but, "Unless she remembers them, I'm keeping the rest."

Another friend of mine glimpsed her two stepdaughters descending upon her like vultures. They didn't ask, "What is Dad's?" "What would you like?" They just swept his room and his workshop clean. No thanks were uttered for the tender loving care she gave their father the last months of his life. For the joy he knew in his last years because of his marriage to her. The man's brother was different. He told the widow he appreciated her efforts.

I'll admit I know little about families. I was an only child. My father's parents were dead long before I was born. My mother was the only one of her family who ever went more than fifty miles from the old farm. Our contacts with relatives were few.

My widower husband had two girls. Both out on their
own when he died. They have been wonderful to me. I've
told them I will try to be as their own mother. Their
children call me "Grandma." I love it, and I adore them. I
believe the feeling is mutual. It's true I'm the only
"maternal" grandmother they've ever known. For the wee
one, the only grandparent she'll see on this earth.

I've given the youngest daughter a traditional wedding.
She expected to take care of it herself—just go to the
parsonage. Her father and I would have enjoyed giving it
to her together, so why shouldn't *I*? Yes, I did it because it
was the right thing, but, more than that, I love her. I
wanted to do it.

Some families are easier to love than others, but, as
Christians, we must do our best.

We must also safeguard our assets, should any remain
at our death. My lawyer gave me some advice that is good
even if we love and trust our families.

"Don't put anyone's name on any bank account of over
$1,000," he told me. "Without your knowledge they can
withdraw the money. At your death they can claim it and
others be left without their fair share."

Also, there are divorces and remarriages among
children. If this happens to one of yours, to protect your
own grandchildren see your lawyer. You don't want them
cut off should your flesh and blood die first. Your child's
assets might revert to the spouse and, ultimately, to the
mate's children of another union. "Protect your own," he
told me.

Sometimes necessity forces families to double up. If you

must live with other members of your family, try to do it peaceably. When my mother-in-law, because of a stroke, moved in with us she tried to do little things to help. She carried out the wastepaper and the garbage. She draped a tea towel over her bad hand, picked up the dish with her good one, and tried to push the towel about the dish. We laughed good-naturedly when the cloth slid off. She attempted many things.

She was totally unlike another widow who, although healthy, waited for her fourteen-year-old granddaughter to get home from school so the girl would fix lunch. She could easily have had the lunch ready for the child. Also, the day after one of her daughters broke a leg, the widow claimed she was too weak to come down the stairs to eat. The daughter struggled up a narrow staircase, cast on her leg and tray in her hands, to enable the mother to partake of some nourishment.

In spite of such situations as I have described, love your family. Try to be helpful. Respect and appreciate their needs.

Love your friends.

As I've mentioned before, their calls may not be as frequent as you'd like, and some may omit you from couples' get-to-gethers, but friendship is a two-way street. How often have you called them? Have you invited them to your home? Have you asked them to ride with you in your car, if you have one? Have you tried to make new friends?

Don't expect to be invited once a week to supper with

them. This wasn't the situation before your husband died.

Don't think they should always pick you up in their car. You shared rides before your husband's death, or you drove to their place. Widowhood doesn't entitle you to "date" privileges.

Don't always give them a résumé of your troubles. You didn't do this before you lost your husband.

Try to treat your friends as you did when there were two of you. They will appreciate it, and you will profit by it.

When I decided to leave Chicago, some of my friends, co-workers, and neighbors put me in the "courageous" class. I didn't belong there. I'm not really brave.

Some said, "You're too young to move down there." "Most people will be much older than you." They really meant, "You're throwing away all your chances of getting married again." They didn't know I'm odd, or maybe just lucky, because I've never felt marriage was the only fulfillment for a woman and a *must*. I firmly believe being unmarried and happy is more to be desired than being unhappy and married.

However, since my days of happy spinsterhood I have discovered that nothing—absolutely nothing—can equal being happily married. It is the most wonderful, exciting, give-and-take world you can live in. God meant it to be that way. I would give almost anything to have my husband back beside me, healthy and forceful.

That isn't to be. Not for me or for you.

This doesn't mean we should dash out and try to find

another man. Some do and are successful at it and happy because of it. I know some of these people, and so do you. However, waiting may prove wiser.

My husband and several other widowed males told me what it's like out there. They've mentioned women who literally throw themselves at a widower.

Of course, men are egotists. Some of them. Any friendly gesture a woman puts forth they translate, "She's after me." According to my sources, however, this is often too true. She *is* after him. *Any* him.

They tell me some are subtle. Some are definitely not. Some want marriage. Some couldn't care less. Most are widowed and lonely themselves. Some have never married. Some — yes — some are even married.

A recent acquaintance asked me why I wouldn't have a romance, an affair, with a married man. She is. His wife doesn't understand him. Perhaps it's true. I think I know why some men are not happily married. I wouldn't want to be married to some women. However, this would never make it right for me.

My acquaintance is finding this satisfies her. It's apparently what she wants or needs. As for me, and not just because I'm a Christian, I couldn't do it. If I knew the man was married, I would always see the wife standing beside him. Never would I be able to forget how I would tear up inside with anguish if someone did this to me, even if I deserved it. Even if I wasn't a good wife.

Besides, I need and want more than that. And you should, too. I must have either a life by myself or *all* the joys, privileges, and problems of loving and being loved by someone who belongs to me alone.

Until my widowhood I would cry over a book or a movie, but never over my own troubles. Now, like many other widows, I know what it is to blink my eyes quickly. Surreptitiously wipe a sudden tear. Clear my throat. Because of a chance word, a similar face, a song. Oh, the tears don't splash down my cheeks, but moisture suddenly fills my eyes at some inconsequential, sometimes unknown, thing. Another man might eliminate this.

I'll admit, too, that I have felt as though I trudged along in a strange country, across a barren field. No trees, no grass, only stone and dust. Another man might shatter this desolate feeling.

But when I have this feeling, I look away. I gaze upward.

My widowed friends tell me it gets worse, not better, as time goes by. They may be right. I may be only a "cockeyed optimist".

A single friend took me to dinner and told me she hoped I wouldn't close my mind to remarriage. Long ago I learned never to say "never."

Some "date" chances have come my way. In the first instance, a friend asked if I would be willing to go to dinner with her and her husband and be the partner of a visiting, recently widowed friend. I went. I had an enjoyable time. But in the back of my mind I knew I was safe. He would be returning to his distant home.

Then an elderly, recently widowed man asked me out. He said he was lonesome on Sundays. I'd known his wife.

Though he is a fine person, he is old enough to be my father. I'm not interested in dating him, but I felt sorry for him. I told him we'd be glad to include him that Sunday in our group on a dutch-treat basis.

Some excitement entered my life when a gentleman saw my picture in the paper and twice came to a church service expecting to meet me. Somehow I couldn't bring myself to say yes to his date proposal. I didn't "know" him.

I'm silly, I know, but, as I went back over these offers, trying to analyze my reactions, I realized I acted the way I did before my marriage. Then, too, I accepted a few "safe" ones. I refused the "old enough to be my father" ones and the dates proposed by men and boys I didn't know.

Maybe that's why it took me so long to find Mr. Right. If so, he was worth waiting for in the past; and, as God leads me, he'll be worth waiting for if one is in my future.

God led one of my friends to three Mr. Rights. The first, she says, was love at first sight. The father of her children. Surviving two heart attacks at age forty, he was seemingly fit, working every day, and even put in a full day of work at the time he died, six years later.

Though friends urged her to meet their eligible men, she determined never to marry until the children were out of high school. Sure her oldest, eighteen, should remain in college, she accepted the counsel of her husband's company and arranged to take her death benefit in monthly installments and accepted a job they offered her. In this way, with the odd jobs the children got, she made it alone until her youngest boy was scheduled to graduate from high school.

Oh, she dated but she felt the children were her first responsibility. "They needed all of me, not a part of me," she said.

When Rob was in his senior year, Claude entered her life. He proved to be another Mr. Right. "A real gentleman and extremely kind to me. My youngest son loved him, and Claude treated him like a prize possession."

This happiness was short-lived. A year after their wedding day Claude entered the hospital for emergency surgery. Four months and two operations later, he was dead.

"To see him suffer four months was the most heartbreaking part of my life, and I knew I would rather see some loved one go suddenly than to see him suffer."

Her last child entered college. She was alone.

"Working, I again joined the Sweet Adelines, an association of women's barbershop quartets. This, with my church work, kept my head high. Friends again introduced me to eligibles, but, feeling I was 'bad luck' for men, I was determined to stay single and enjoy my grandchildren.

"God's plan for me was not so, and I again met a Christian man . . . and have been happily married eleven years."

Her third Mr. Right, active in his church, fitted in beautifully with her way of life. "We attend all activities together and have a true feeling of oneness."

Her "another man" advice is to "only meet eligible men through *trusted* friends—*not* at bars, bowling halls, and such."

She also recommends—and it's her first recommendation for widows—"Always have faith in the Lord; he will not let you down."

Her way of attracting men was more of a "fleeing" method, but do you remember some of the stupid things we tried when boys first interested us? My seventy-year-old neighbor has joined in laughter over some good-natured teasing we've given her.

She helped serve when her circle hosted a church dinner. One of her arthritic fingers suddenly gave way, and she spilled coffee on the sleeve of a recent widower. A few days later he called her.

On our way to the event she was gratified to have as a reason for refusing his date offer, she admitted she needed our advice. She felt sure he would call again. And he did.

She followed our instructions, and they spent a pleasant evening together. She is very attractive and looks at least ten years younger than her three score and ten. When age entered the conversation she was honest. She is several years his senior, and that was the last date invitation she received from him.

Honesty is important in dating. Our own matchmaker said she never knew two people so honest with each other. The second day I lunched with Cliff I told him I couldn't cook. He didn't really believe it until he observed me preparing to put grease in the skillet to fry bacon at our first breakfast in our honeymoon cottage.

Frankness is usually easier the second time around.

One of my young friends said she felt like a schoolgirl, preparing for her first date after her husband's death. "I found that being yourself is the best way," she says. "It's too much of an effort to put up a false front if you date one person for any length of time. You want a person to like you for what you are."

One of her first dates married her. However, he knew from the start that there were two little boys at her house. She kept no surprises for him. "God wants us to be honest in all our relationships with others. It's paid off for me."

A young widowed friend recently remarried. At first she was sure she would never love again. It hurt her dreadfully when some of her married friends suspected she had designs on their husbands.

The first time it happened, Lisa just wanted to go to a John Wayne movie. Tom wanted to, too. His wife didn't.

"I'd love to see it if you won't mind me tagging along," Lisa said as they sat on the patio talking.

"I'll go with Tom, or he will go alone," his wife quietly replied.

Later, at home, Lisa remembered those quiet, simple words. And the true meaning came across loud and clear. She knew she was innocent of any ulterior motive. She just wanted to see John Wayne, and her spontaneity had carried her onto dangerous ground.

"From then on, I watched what I said," Lisa told me.

"On another occasion a third party clued me in that the wife of one of the couples in the complex was 'watching' me," Lisa mentioned. This couple were new friends but had been bulwarks for her.

Not knowing if the third party was just trying to start trouble, Lisa asked the wife to come over. She frankly told her about the accusation and honestly explained she was not after the husband. Then she asked the husband to join them and filled him in.

"Such a talk, preceded by prayer, is the better way to handle this type of situation," Lisa believes.

As a result of these happenings she learned to do more previously classified "men" things for herself, in order to depend less on the husbands of friends.

Lisa has some tips for you young widows, and we'll let you older ones listen.

1. Do not go anywhere too frequently when a friend's husband will be there.
2. If you must use the other woman's husband, or talk to him, or have him over to fix something, never exclude the wife. Tell her the coffeepot is on, to plan to come, too. That way the choice is hers.
3. I Thessalonians 5:22: "Abstain from all appearance of evil."

As often happens to young widows, friends tried to do some matchmaking. It didn't work for Lisa.

At a Halloween party at a neighbors she met Bob. He walked her around the corner to her home. He called, later, for a date. She didn't intend to get involved, but most women enjoy an occasional night out, no strings attached.

As they began to see each other on a friendly basis, she noticed how good he was to her children. He included them in many outings. He was easy to be with. He made her feel comfortable. She began to look forward to his calls. To seeing him. To going to church together.

Often when they were with her family, her dead husband was mentioned. She felt it made things tense for him. So she talked it out with him and asked him to try to overlook it, if possible.

Her mother-in-law was delighted with Bob. Thrilled that she had met someone so kind.

As the days went by, friendship changed to love. Then came the day when they must tell her parents—and her late husband's mother. It was easier than she thought it would be. They never shut out her first mother-in-law. In fact, she considers Bob as a son she has gained in her own son's place.

Now not only is Lisa living again but she has found a new love, a new marriage. She is fortunate. She has found a man who loves not only her but also her children. The oldest is young enough that his memory of his flesh-and-blood father is hazy, and the little one was born after the father's death.

The pressure of children makes the request for God's leading of even greater importance in your life.

Friends of mine adopted a boy whose mother remarried when he was two. When his two sisters were born his mother found she was shielding him more and more from the anger of his stepfather. After her illness and early death, the stepfather packed up and left with his two girls, abandoning the boy. The lad was six at the time. It has left its mark on his life.

If you have children and are thinking about remarriage, be certain God is leading you in that direction. If he is, it can be a marvelous thing for all of you.

Sometimes the story is in the reverse. Both of my husband's daughters wanted him to remarry. One was married herself. The other was a teen-ager and at home.

My crepe-hanging friends wondered if I wasn't scared at the prospect. I guess I didn't have sense enough to worry, as I knew marriage to Cliff was the Lord's plan for me.

My adjustment to the oldest girl was easiest. She and her husband have always lived over three hundred miles from us, and we saw them only several times a year. A granddaughter arrived eight months and three days after our marriage, and her coming helped. The daughter saw how enchanted I was with Cindy, and I'm sure this cemented our relationship from the beginning.

The younger daughter had emotional problems. She was tall for her age and had always been overweight. Since she was her mother's favorite, the sudden shock of her mother's death was doubly trying.

Perhaps I'm not a good example of what a stepmother should be. I continued working, so I did not spend a lot of time with her. I tried to penetrate her heart, and sometimes I got excited as she would gab away to me. But the next day she would ignore me. But then, she ignored nearly everyone.

When she moved to her own place, I'll admit I was relieved. One of the few arguments my husband and I ever had was over her. That day I spilled out all the pent-up feelings of nearly ten years. Whether he spoke to her or whether she began to realize, when she was on her own, what both of us had done for her, I'll probably never know; but the relationship began to change.

She was a bulwark to me in his last illness. I feel we are now very close. I love her dearly, and have from the first.

If you decide God is leading you to remarriage, and there are children—his children—involved, don't expect heaven. It rarely happens that way. You must work at it in love.

When children are involved, his or yours, a will is a necessity. For both of you. My husband doubted me the day I told him this. The lawyer agreed with me.

You see, if one of you outlives the other by even a minute, without a will the estate goes to the family of the survivor. Had this happened to us, it would have been possible for all my never-seen cousins and other distant relatives to lay claim to what should have gone to his daughters. A premarital agreement is not always just a tool of the rich. It may be a wise thing for you to consider.

Occasionally there are aged parents to be thought of.

I shall never forget the unease of spirit that accompanied a friend as we drove to move her mother from a distant point to a place closer to her. She had remarried and knew that her mother and husband didn't like each other.

Another friend has solved the problem by insisting her brothers and sisters take the mother on weekends. This is not possible if you are an only child or live far removed from relatives.

Even though nursing and retirement homes are greatly improved today, there is still hesitance in forcing a parent to enter one.

Each of us has different problems to solve. But this

doesn't bother God. He's big enough to help everyone of us if we rely on him.

So don't close the door to dating again, to remarriage. But keep God as your Guide and don't leap into something just because you are sad and lonely. Give even love time to flower again in your life.

Just as I never thought I was the marrying kind in the first place, I do not anticipate finding another man or another marriage.

I know it happens. I know the results can be very good. I'm not saying "never." Neither should you. If the added dividend of a fine Christian man enters your life, don't be afraid to love again. My husband always said. "To want to love again and marry is a compliment to marriage."

10

A Very Special Person

Widow, you are a very special person.

The most basic feelings God ever gave man have honed every nerve and fiber of your being to exquisite sharpness. You know what it means to be swept along by love, dashed to the lowest depths of despair. You have scaled the highest pinnacle of exultation and descended into still, lovely pools of reflection and complete peace.

The present surges around you. Offering the greatest choices of life, the most freedom you will ever know.

The road ahead points to the stars.

Look back.

Think of the tingling sensation that started somewhere and flooded your being from the top of your head to the tips of your toes every time you saw him approaching. I remember.

The sparkle in your eyes that makes every bride beautiful was there. I know the starry twinkle was in my eyes for everyone to observe.

You have known the peak of emotion reached as you two became one flesh and the blissful quietness that followed. Sublime feelings. These have been yours and mine.

True, we have also known the depths of despair. The

lost, alone feeling of separation. But isn't it this experience that heightens the memories of all the love and laughter and loyalty we have shared?

Look back. Don't be afraid. Don't try to close the past out of your life. Life has been good. Exciting. Full of unforgettable moments.

Tennyson knew what he was saying when he wrote:

> 'Tis better to have loved and lost
> Than never to have loved at all.

Then look ahead. The road points to the stars. I believe that. And, I'm reaching for those stars.

A widow living in one of the smallest rooms in a home for the aged is one of the most "look ahead" women I know. She is in charge of the wardrobe for the residents. She gaily looks forward to each arrival of donated clothes. She separates them and puts them in the proper place. She helps other residents pick out what they need and choose the most flattering things.

From the small pocket money she is given each month, she manages to tithe to the church and to save something so that she can invite a friend to visit her for lunch.

She is often dizzy and must rest occasionally each day. Arthritis and poor eyesight are only minor barriers to letter writing. She can always find someone willing to address the envelope, and the large, shaky, irregular handwriting inside is happily deciphered by her friends. At ninety-three, after over sixteen years in this home, she is still one of the happiest widows I know.

So, look ahead.

This year I have reveled in three springs. Two totally unexpected at the year's beginning.

I expected the rosy aura of the redbud, the dainty pink and white blooms of the dogwood, and the yellow gold of the forsythia, which proclaim spring has arrived in the Ozarks. The azaleas and camelias of Natchez, New Orleans, and Florida were an unexpected dividend. But in my wildest dreams, I didn't foresee the rhododendron, double white lilacs, wild fuchsias, golden rain trees, and the yellow gorse of Ireland, let alone the bluebells of Scotland and the fragrant May blossoms of England.

As a widow I can pick up and leave at the drop of a hat. A friend says, "Let's go," and I go. A relative says "Come," and I arrive.

The typewriter's clatter, the reading lamp's beams bother no one no matter the hour. When the clothes are dirty, I wash. When the buffet is dusty, I dust. I vacuum, scrub, and garden at will. I'm my own woman. Not bossed, dominated, pushed . . . or loved.

But I'm looking ahead. To other trips. To more successful books, articles, and stories. To new places to sing and speak. To grasping wonderful friends to my soul with hoops of steel.

Think of the untried battlefields before you. Look ahead. The road is pointing to the stars.

And, don't forget—be sure to look up.

Remember your Maker, who only giveth good things.

Who takes your hand and leads you. Sometimes beside troubled waters. Who has led him, your husband, *through* the shadow of death into the eternal light and love of heaven. Who will never forsake you.

Widow, you are a very special person.

Appendix

Here are some planning suggestions for those readers who are not widows.

One of the first things you should do is buy a personal records ledger at your stationer's. (Some companies provide similar booklets for their employees.) Fill it in as completely as possible.

When such a ledger is filled in, it will give you very adequate information on:

1. Employment benefits
2. Social Security information
3. Where proofs of age and marriage certificates are kept
4. Information on bank, savings and loan, and credit union accounts
5. Insurance information on:
   a. Self
   b. Spouse
   c. Dependents
   d. House
   e. Health
   f. Automobile
   g. Other

6. Savings bond and stocks and bond information
7. Real estate owned, mortgage, taxes, and insurance coverage
8. Safe deposit box and what it contains
9. Wills and cemetery lots, executor's name, attorney's name
10. Financial obligations
11. Other important papers
12. Professional advisers and closest friends and relatives
13. Important dates
14. Your own personal notes

THINGS YOU SHOULD KNOW

1. Have knowledge of some skill (typing, teaching, bookkeeping, otherwise) so you can earn a living if widowed.
2. Know how to drive a car if one is available.
3. Know your own and your spouse's wishes in case of death: where you are to be buried; if you are to be cremated; whether you wish to donate any of your organs to science; whether you want an autopsy performed (a complete one is not necessary; it can be restricted to certain areas of the body).
4. Know how to balance a checking account; how to obtain cash; etc.
5. Be aware of when taxes, insurance, etc., are due.
6. Know how to keep a budget.

7. Have a burial plot. They are relatively easy to sell if you move before it's needed.

8. Have a will, especially if:
   a. You are married to a widower or widow.
   b. Your spouse has children by a previous partner.
   c. You have children you wish to protect by an inheritance.
   d. If any of your sons or daughters are married to someone who has children by another mate. (Your will can be set up to protect your flesh-and-blood grandchildren.)
   e. Have a will even if none of the above apply.

P.S. Stay *alive* the rest of your life. And may God grant you a happy life together, no matter how long.